Completely Revised

Part I
A *New* SENSORY Self-Awareness

Practice Guide for School, Work, and Home

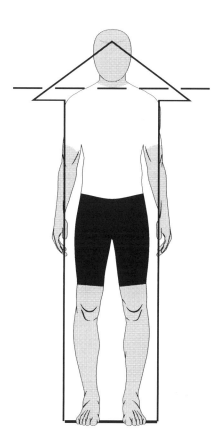

Tools to Experience
The Body-to-Brain Communication

Catherine Rosasco Mitchell
Introduction by Carla Hannaford, Ph.D.

©2012, 2013 by Catherine Rosasco Mitchell

All rights reserved, including the right to reproduce this book or portions thereof in any form whatsoever. For information contact: Feldenkrais Interest, P.O. Box 6934, Kamuela, HI 96743, info@FeldenkraisInterest.com.

ISBN-13:
978-0615689371 (Wellness Through Movement®)

ISBN-10:
061568937X

Cover design by Barrie Rose, interior graphics by Andriy Yankovsky

This book is dedicated
to "our" children
and
to my father Andrew Rosasco

TABLE OF CONTENTS

PREFACE

This book is designed to build a bridge from traditional education (focusing attention "out there" for learning) to learning from within - to understanding "who" is the learner. Learning is a whole body experience; in the nervous system – though we may not be able to feel it – the body sends more information up to the brain than comes from the brain to the body.

Awareness of this understanding of how the body influences thinking and perception can only happen through experience. Though there are many scientific references, words in a book cannot explain this experience; scientific or literary explanations simply do not "make sense." To borrow Albert Einstein's analogy: It would be like describing the power of a Beethoven symphony as "particles of wave variables displayed on a graph." Just as the feeling of hearing a symphony can never be described in words, *Sensory Self-Awareness* must be experienced.

"Sensations" are what digest thinking, contemplate feeling, and change learning into understanding. These lessons will show participants, regardless of age or condition, ***how*** the pattern (symphony) of bodily sensations influences thinking. The lessons lead to an awareness of the physical sensations in the character of attitude that connect perspective of perception and the behavior of "how" we learn.

Understanding the power of this phenomenon comes only after experience. The sensations of the body, strongly or softly, indirectly or directly, influence perception. The awareness of this interplay gives insights that have changed tens of thousands of lives.

Who Should Read this Book

- People who want to raise or teach children from the heart as well as the intellect
- People who are young and just starting school
- People who are learning new concepts
- People who have reoccurring challenges with communication
- People who have little time to themselves for introspection
- People who want to strengthen their understanding of guidance from within
- People who have difficulty deciding what is best for them and the good of all
- People who have chronic health issues and don't know why
- People who are losing mobility and balance
- People who are living in crowded spaces

Experiencing the lessons explains more than words could ever convey.

ACKNOWLEDGMENTS

Writing this book has been one of the most humbling experiences of my life. There are so many big-hearted people in our community who put so much time into creating this program, but one name not on the cover (although it should be) is Jo Piltz. Without Jo, this book would *never* have been possible. I'm forever grateful for her long hours, diligent heart, and artistic ability as my editor. Gratitude also goes to grand finale editors, Susan Switzer and Barbara Abramson; to graphic magician Barrie Rose for the cover design; and to Audriy Yankovsky for interior graphics.

Then there is *my* teacher… Moshe Feldenkrais bridged the science of physics (of the physical body) into the dimensions of consciousness and how we learn. Mahalo Dr. Feldenkrais for enriching my life forever.

Esther Hughes, Doug Connors, and Jody Lubrecht, for your years of weekly guidance in how to align with the Department of Education and with the federal and state education regulations, and Pat Linton, for putting this team together, I thank you.

Special thanks to Principal Garcia, Kohala Elementary School, for his courage to break new ground in the hearts and minds of a school environment and his enthusiasm about the program with teachers, students, and parents. Thanks also to Art Souza, Superintendent of the County of Hawaii, for helping us understand how to make the program easier for school communities to adapt these lessons. Nancy (Cat) Jones, thank you for your passion and curiosity that blazed the path in how to become a *Wellness Through Movement*® teacher.

I want to give a warm mahalo to the many people in the writer's ohana, *Waimea Writers Group*, especially Greer Sucke, Jim Cisler, Wanda Patterson, John Holland, and Dave Fouts, for all the years of encouragement and critical analysis.

Susie Jones, your heart is precious. Susie, a former physical education teacher at Hawaii Preparatory Academy (HPA), initiated this venture and helped put the content of this program together. Without Susie, the "element" of fun would have suffered, and as a result the program would never have survived. HPA opened their doors and supplied equipment, space, and the professional expertise of their staff, specifically instructional leader and elementary educator Hope Soo.

Deep gratitude goes to the Hawaii Island community: the parents, children, and teachers who took time out of their busy schedules to give us feedback and try out the lessons. Donna Rohr, teacher at Parker Elementary School, your painstaking efforts in trying out the first drafts of the lessons demonstrate the enthusiasm and perseverance you have in addition to being a full-time teacher. Gratitude also goes to Eva Conway at Kohala Elementary for letting us bring *Wellness Through Movement*® into her classroom and testing results with academic studies. After working with her class, the program turned into a three-part series; the first part designed for the general public.

John Mitchell, my loving and supportive husband, thank you for your patience and compassion during the seven years of testing and revising this program. Friends Patty Bigelow, Lydia Deems, Bill Prothero, and Kiki Corbin, thank you for being there to catch me with words of encouragement when I fell. I treasure you all.

The people of the Hawaiian communities, something deep inside, and a muse made of grace wrote this program, and I want to say…

Mahalo Nui Loa for your aloha.

Catherine Rosasco Mitchell

FOREWORD

You are so fortunate to have in your hands this manual, *Part I: A New Self-Awareness*, the first section of Catherine Rosasco-Mitchell's three-part *Wellness Through Movement®* masterwork. This clear set of lessons is based on Catherine's deep knowledge of the *Feldenkrais Method®*, her investigation into the sources of sensory awareness, and her thirty years of experience working with clients. Her passion is to enable people of all ages to reach inside themselves and to listen to their own bodies in order to understand their individual perceptions of the world outside. Most recently, Catherine has spent seven years investigating and enriching the lives of children in several schools in Hawaii. This wonderful book is the result of that journey.

Of course, I am pleased to introduce to you my friend Catherine Rosasco Mitchell as a highly educated and dedicated teacher, but so much would be missing from that simple statement. Catherine and I have known each other for years as amateur singers in the Waimea Community Chorus, but only this spring did we become close friends and colleagues. Since she asked me to be her editor, Catherine and I have spent months together over computers and coffee cups, as we struggled, laughed, shared histories, and finally merged our skills in order to produce this wonderful book. In the process, I introduced Catherine to the vagaries of the English language, but she taught me much more important lessons about the value of listening to the messages from within our own bodies that open our minds to where we are and who we are. Although Catherine claimed to need my 40 years of teaching experience to bolster her 30 years of scientific knowledge and practice, I constantly found her to be a truly empathetic and creative teacher who instinctively offers her knowledge to those who need it most.

If you are a teacher or a parent, here is a book with twelve accessible lessons set in enjoyable games and exercises that offer practice in awareness skills that will forever enrich the lives of the children in your care. It is a tool that will easily introduce you and your children to a deeper understanding of the symbiotic relationship between the body and brain, and the supporting material in the appendices offers an additional wealth of explanation of the implications of the most advanced research. Most of all, I envy you the opportunity to meet Catherine, my warm and knowledgeable friend, and to profit from her expertise as you enter her world of Sensory Self-Awareness in the following pages. Enjoy!

Jo Amanti Piltz

INTRODUCTION

A *New* Sensory *Self-Awareness* provides lessons that promote an understanding of the influences the sensory world, both from the environment and our own bodies has on our reality. Although many believe that thinking is only about the brain, neuroanatomist Jill Bolte-Taylor says: "We are feeling creatures that think, not thinking creatures that feel" (Bolte-Taylor, 2006).

Sensations play a much bigger part in how the mind operates than previously believed. Sensations from our heart, gut, and movement patterns have strong effects on our moods, attitudes, and even learning. These sensations are dependent on each other to substantiate our reality, enhance our curiosity about the world and ourselves, and assist us to learn and grow in understanding.

Scientists are finding:
"Realizing that the mind is anchored to the body's actions and surroundings gives us a better understanding of our social behavior, emotional, and cognitive lives."

"The body is our only real tether to the world? All the knowledge we acquire, we get through our senses!"

"Higher cognitive processes are grounded in bodily experience. The brain's low-level sensory and motor circuits do not just feed into cognition, THEY ARE COGNITION!" (Scientific American Mind, Jan./Feb. 2011, p.39-45)

Elementary teachers and parents introduce the world to children, but how do we define "the world"? Is it a stressful and dangerous place in which children are at the mercy of social and academic challenges, their own emotional storms, and those of others? In a world where the leading cause of death of youngsters between the ages of 10 and 24 is suicide, there is greater need than ever for children to balance the rich sensory world within to their outer world. That is the role of *Sensory Self-Awareness*.

The purpose of this program is to enable teachers, students, and their families to learn a *new* kind of self-awareness. The strategies focus attention on the sensory-motor sensations in a mindful way that makes for a greater awareness of "self." Enhancing "sensory mindfulness" produces improved attention span, diminishes aggressive behavior, promotes caring and responsible behavior and is a direct link to optimizing learning and memory in the classroom, at home, and for a lifetime. (Barnes et al. 2003. Napoli et al. 2005. Schonert-Reichl and Miller 2005)

This program gives teachers and parents simple, profound tools to reduce stress, build empathy, lengthen attention span, improve classroom control, and make learning more effective at all levels. Children and teachers who are aware of the body's influence on the brain have a broader and more developed sense of self-awareness; this awareness inspires self-management, improves social relations, opens us to a greater reality, and assists us in developing *Emotional Intelligence* (Coleman).

Scientists are now realizing the vast importance of play, especially imaginative play which applies sensory/motor sensations to learning in a more meaningful way. Because these lessons are fun, they can easily be incorporated into regular classroom lessons and activities, and in the home setting where both parent and child benefit. (See *Appendix A* for more details).

PART I A NEW SENSORY SELF-AWARENESS Tools to Experience Body-to-Brain Communication: This dynamic and interactive series of twelve lessons shows participants how to feel the influence their bodies have on thinking and feeling. The program is designed to improve awareness, in-classroom management, and school culture. Participants learn how to shift perception from outside to inside by developing a clearer sense of self and their relationship with others. An array of self-observing techniques using breath, sound, and movement promote awareness of mental, emotional, and physical interconnections. *A New* Sensory *Self Awareness* helps lives change.

PART II YOUNG AT HEART P.E. For the Heart, Body, and Mind: This in-depth series of twenty neuromuscular reeducation movement games is based on the *Feldenkrais Method®*, developmental movements, and the National Physical Education Standards for elementary grades. The program uses alignment, attitude, and quality of movement to expand perception. Games also target the physical and emotional challenges that narrow attention or fuel problem behaviors. *Young At Heart P.E.* organizes the stimulus of motor patterns that contribute to self-perception.

PART III MOVEMENT FOR THE LEARNER In-Classroom Curriculum: This series of fifty-two in-classroom sensory-movement lessons is designed to enhance brain functioning and improve performance in language arts and mathematics. More important, the lessons aid in developing social skills, attention skills, and higher order skills. These lessons are designed to also increase physical comfort for people while seated at a desk or when they are required to have long attention spans. *Movement for the Learner In-Classroom Curriculum* integrates the studies of the *Feldenkrais Method®*, cognitive development theories, and stages of sensory-motor development.

Note

Part I can be led by anyone skilled in working with groups of children. A one-day introductory workshop is recommended but not required.

Part II requires a trained *Feldenkrais®* practitioner or certified *Wellness Through Movement®* teacher who can work with groups of children.

Part III can be taught by teachers who have also attended a one-week training program. Their children however must have completed *Parts I and II*.

Carla Hannaford, Ph.D.

OVERVIEW

A Bird's Eye View of the Guide and the Lessons

Part I

YOU ARE SENSATIONAL
Philosophy Behind "A New Sensory Self-Awareness"
How Does Sensory Self-Awareness Improve Cognitive Learning?
Sensing How We Learn
Adapting the Learner Academic Curriculum
Teacher and Parental Benefits
Improved Communication, Limited Stress, Higher Academic Achievement
Empathy
Longer Attention Spans and Self-Directed Learners
Dealing with Reoccurring Challenges and Saving Time
Sensory Self-Awareness for Different Ages and Developmental Stages
Sensory Self-Awareness for Health and Obesity
Summary

GETTING STARTED
Recommendations before all lessons
Muscle-Testing for Water, getting children interested in their bodies

LESSON SEQUENCE
Lessons are cumulative. Enjoy the journey!
Level 1   Foundational Lessons
Level 2   Core Lessons
Level 3   All Ages
Level 4   Adults

PART I LESSONS

Lessons are cumulative, organically building awareness to have a direct experience of how sensations influence thoughts.

SUMMARY OF PART I LESSONS

PART I – LESSON 1 Pancake Body

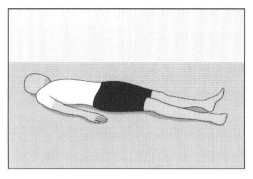

Objective or Movement Intention is to provide a type of biofeedback against the floor from the sensation in our bodies <u>to</u> our brains *and* expand awareness of the connections between physical sensations, feeling, and thinking.

Background Behind the Lesson:
When participants have a clear sense of subtle sensations in their bodies - which come from their proprioceptive or kinesthetic sense - they can easily connect the influence of subtle physical sensations to mental or emotional perceptions. Charles Sherrington, winner of the Nobel Prize in Physiology, described this as a "sixth sense."

PART I – LESSON 2 Personal Bubbles Freeze Dance

Objective or Movement Intention is to increase spatial and perceptual awareness of self and others, the core movement of spiral rotation through the spine, and the virtue of respect. Emphasis is on teaching the ability to have attention (shifting perception) on both the visceral (inward) and (outward) awareness. (Respect self and others)

Background Behind the Lesson:
There are three types of personal space: One involves exteroceptive perception, the external spherical or personal feeling space; the second is interoceptive perception, perceives pain and stretching; and the third, focuses on proprioception, which deals with the personal space that gives feedback on the status within the body. This lesson focuses on the third.

Research at the Institute of HeartMath demonstrates that the heart generates the strongest rhythmic electromagnetic field in the body; the heart space of this field extends ten feet in diameter around a person. This electromagnetic field is virtually a "bubble" surrounding the body.

PART I – LESSON 3 <u>Personal Bubbles & No Place Like Home Breath</u>

Objective or Movement Intention is to develop self-awareness through the sensations of proprioception, to focus the ability to change what is perceived, and to learn breathing strategies that center the mind and body.

Background Behind the Lesson:
"Only when a child must, in some way, change what he perceives around him is logical thinking involved," according to Celia Lavatelli's book, *Piaget's Theory of Development* (Lavatelli, 1973).

A *Personal Bubble* is similar to the energetic or magnetic field (which scientists have measured with biofeedback machines) that surrounds the body and emanates from the heart. Finding the boundary of this field can help individuals find their center; feeling the difference between the outer space and the center is the nature of how the nervous system learns.

PART I – LESSON 4 <u>No Place Like Home Breath</u>

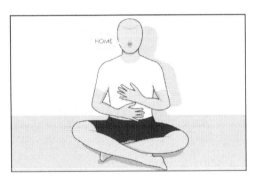

Objective or Movement Intention is to become aware of how breathing techniques can center the mind and to use the interior sensations of inhalations and exhalations to bring attention inside.

Background Behind the Lesson:
Long exhalations slow the heart rate and can center and calm the mind and nervous system. This type of breathing can serve as a tool to release tension and stress. Exhaling deeply sends messages to the vagus nerve and can help calm the heart rate. The information from the aortic body (aortic means in relation to the orifice of the left ventricle of the heart) travels along the vagus nerve (the tenth cranial nerve) to the respiratory (breathing) center. "The vagus nerve contains thousands of nerve fibers, many of which also carry information from the heart to the brain" (Childre & Martin, 1999, p. 31).

PART I – LESSON 5 Big Tiny Bubbles

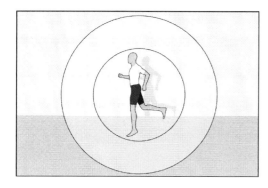

Objective or Movement Intention is to develop awareness of differences in space and level of spatial awareness in relationship to the body, to others, and to the environment.

Background Behind the Lesson:
Alternating awareness from inside to the environment is another way our biological nature teaches us our relationship to ourselves and to the world around us. The ability to integrate both perspectives is foundational for how we learn as individuals. Alternating attention within and outside the body also integrates intention and action.

PART I – LESSON 6 Listening Bubbles

Objective or Movement Intention is to associate the sense of physical space to sound and increase respect toward others while speaking.

Background Behind the Lesson:
"Listening" may be a challenge due to a loud internal dialogue of anxiety or to physical discomfort. Researchers Alfred Tomatis and Christian Vold are switching their focus more to the problems of listening than hearing.

A good deal of brain activity is the work of "silent" traffic, involuntary processes of function from the bodily metabolism to a complex matrix of perceptions integrating taste, smell, touch, proprioception, and so on. (Robinson, 2001, p. 99) The exploration of the internal dialogue of private perceptions is a crucial element in creativity.

PART I – LESSON 7 _Body Bubbles_

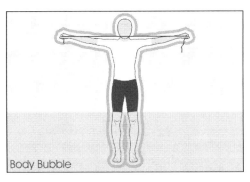

Body Bubble

Objective or Movement Intention is to expand awareness of the proprioceptive sense (the body's orientation within itself, the space around the body, and the 19 senses).

Background Behind the Lesson:
There are three types of personal space: One involves exteroceptive perception, the external spherical or personal feeling space; the second is interoceptive perception, perceives pain and stretching; and the third, focuses on proprioception, which deals with the personal space that gives feedback on the status within the body. This lesson focuses on the third.

PART I – LESSON 8 _Hokey Pokey Body Bubble_

Objective or Movement Intention is to increase self-awareness of how parts of the body work as a whole and to create a clearer sense of balance and wholeness in space inside and outside the body.

Background Behind the Lesson:
Sensing equal and opposites sides such as the six cardinal directions (1. Right, 2. Left, 3. Front, 4. Back, 5. Above, 6. Below) is what the nervous system constantly does to find balance and coordination. Over 19 senses send signals between the body and the brain. "Signals from this sensory motor orchestration are sent by afferent nerves through the spinal cord to the somatosensory, motor and parietal cortices of the brain, where they continuously feed and update dynamic sensory-motor maps of the body" (Smetacek & Mechsner, 2004, p. 21).

PART I – LESSON 9 Dancin' Hula Hoops

Objective or Movement Intention is to improve spatial awareness within the body, soften the deep, intricate articulations of the spine and torso, and increase spatial awareness between the body and environment. (A spiral rotation of movement vertical to gravity is a foundational movement to all of life.)

Background Behind the Lesson:
Having attention to hula hoops spinning around the body magnifies spatial awareness around the body and thus the orientation of proprioceptive awareness. The proprioceptive sense orients the relationship of body parts in space. "In 1906, Charles Sherrington (1857-1952) coined the term proprioception (perception of one's own self)…and called it our 'secret sixth sense.' However, this concept of the body as a major sense organ has failed to arouse the interest it deserves." Proprioceptors precisely measure physical properties, such as muscle length, tendon tension, joint angle or deep pressure. (Smetacek & Mechsner, 2004, p. 21)

PART I – LESSON 10 Hula Relay Personal Bubbles

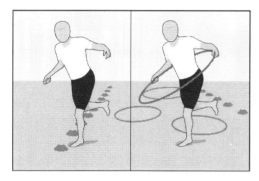

Objective or Movement intention is to improve spatial awareness within and around the body, integrate moving of spiral rotation, develop more respect for others, and use math skills to help in daily interactions.

Background Behind the Lesson:
Hula hooping creates spatial awareness challenges, which can deepen proprioceptive awareness and integrate core muscles for spiral rotation - a primary motion for developmental movement sequences in the first year of life. The proprioceptive sense orients the relationship of body parts in space. In 1906, Charles Sherrington (1857 – 1952) coined the term 'proprioception' (perception of one's own self), and called it our 'secret sixth sense.' But this concept of the body as a major sense organ has failed to arouse the interest it deserves.

PART I – LESSON 11 Ho'oponopono Home

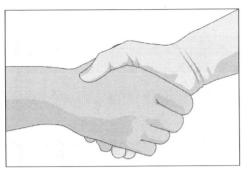

Objective or Movement Intention is to improve communication and social skills through body-to-mind conflict resolution strategies.

Background Behind the Lesson:
This lesson is based on the teachings of ho'oponopono, *Home Breath* lessons, *and Non-Violent Communication* techniques by Marshall Rosenberg. The dynamics that happen among people and the dynamics that happen among parts of ourselves are similar. The effect *Ho'oponopono Home* has on people is similar to the way habitual patterning affects muscular skeletal patterns. Habitual patterns in muscles mirror the behavior of the brain. *Hooponopono Home* enhances compassion between people when the listener repeats (mirrors) what was said *by* the speaker in a way that reaches the heart *of the speaker.*

PART I – LESSON 12 Over, Under, Around

Objective or Movement Intention is to associate thinking with physical sensation, improve awareness around and inside the body, and orient awareness to the six cardinal directions.

Background Behind the Lesson:
Perception is related to physical space in and around the body and how we orient ourselves to the environment. The interpretation of the directions gives insight on how we think subconsciously in relationship with our world. In formal education, we are trained to put all our attention outside of ourselves, with very little training directed to attention inside. The most important reason these lessons were created was to direct attention inside.

Appendix A
NOTES AND BACKGROUND

Why We Do Each Step in the Lesson: To re-educate patterns of sensations
Background Behind Each Lesson: Relevant research in sensations and perception

Appendix B
SUPPORTING SCHOOL NEEDS

Specific school needs that lessons support:

Attention
  Attention
  Focus
  Listening
Developmental
Higher Order
  Cross Lateral Movements
  Self-Awareness
  Self-Awareness with Others
  Spatial Awareness of Body
  Spatial Awareness of Others
Math
  Addition and Subtraction
  Geometry
  Spatial Awareness
  Symmetry
Memory
Neuromuscular Re-education
  Neuromuscular Re-education
  Alignment

Social
  Communication Skills
  Conflict Resolution
  Discipline
  Respect
  Safety
  Social Behavior
  Teamwork
Stress Reduction
  Calming
  Centering
  Recharge
  Relaxation
  Self-Awareness
  Stress Reduction
Transition Times
  Passive
  Active

"It would be possible to describe everything scientifically, but it would make no sense; it would be without meaning, as if we could describe a Beethoven symphony as a variation of wave pressure."

—Albert Einstein

YOu ARE SENSATIONAL

Philosophy Behind "A New Sensory Self-Awareness"

When a group of seventeen writers were asked to describe the terms "self awareness" and "sensory," no two people answered the same way. Responses ranged from "Self-awareness is being selfish" to "Self awareness is being aware of your potential and what you are capable of doing" to "Self awareness is the infinite self." The writers defined the word "sensory" as having to do with the five senses and what they do, such as smelling, seeing, hearing etc., or as an awareness of "everything out there and *around* us."

These varying definitions are a reflection of current consciousness and perception. "Sensory" and "self-awareness" however, do not operate separately; the two words cannot be divided from each other. Scientists are now finding that "sensory" and "self-awareness" are inseparable.

Anthropologists understand that people's perceptions of "self-awareness" and "sensory" are not associated. Thus, they describe "awareness" from four different perspectives:

1. Awareness of physical form (our bodies)
2. Awareness of mind and body as separate entities (Western medicine model)
3. Awareness of mind, body, and heart as inseparable.
4. Awareness of mind, body, heart, and *spirit* as inseparable.

This book describes the third perspective - the symbiotic connection of mind, body, and heart – and how to develop that awareness.

Our bodies and minds have not changed, but in today's science, our understanding of the symbiotic relationship between body and mind is changing. Therefore, what is taught in the fields of education and medicine is subject to change.

As recently as the 1960's, Jean Piaget, developer of what many consider the reigning theories in elementary education, suggested that the *perceptual* process and the *operational* process are two separate processes: "Training in perceptual skills (self-awareness) will not lead to the transformation of data essential to logical thinking." However, he also believed "...a child's intellectual competence involves levels of motivation and self concept" (Lavatelli, 1973).

Did Piaget think levels of motivation and self-concept are separate from the physiology of our senses that form perception? In 1906, Charles Sherrington, Nobel Prize winning neurophysiologist at Yale University, referenced another sense that gives us "one's own perception." Dr. John Ratey, of Harvard University, says that the old paradigm of the "human need to divide and conquer, to separate out two kingdoms" is fading and that "separating the body and the brain is rapidly coming to be seen as ridiculous" (Ratey, 2001).

The paradigm of educational science is shifting as brain research bridges neurology with physiology and psychology.

Sally Goddard, at the Institute of Neuro Physiological Psychology, in her book *Teacher's Window Into the Child's Mind,* states that researchers in the 1970's knew "specific movements would cause changes in the brain" (Goddard, 1996).

The *Feldenkrais Method®,* designed by physicist Moshe Feldenkrais, deals with the inseparable infusion of mind and body measured by qualities of motion. This method is getting more and more support from scholars in the fields of neurology, physical therapy, and psychology. Psychologists today study perception *with* sensory awareness (Goldstein, 1995), and educational scientists also recognize that the many sources of human capabilities are derived not just from the brain but also from multiple intelligences within the body (Gardner, 1999; Childre and Martin, 1999). Intelligence testing is undoubtedly changing as we learn more about the human brain.

In the 1870's, Francis Galton measured Intelligence Quotient (I.Q.) by sensory acuity (Gardner, 1999). Sensory acuity is the ability to notice subtle changes in levels of brightness, in weight and degrees of pressure, and even levels of sound. Now, although scientific proof does not yet exist, scholars are interested in how the body affects perception.

How does Sensory Self-Awareness Improve Cognitive Learning?

To understand *how* the mental process of cognitive development improves through 'self-awareness," the terms "sensory" and "self-awareness" need to be redefined. We often use the same terms to say something different. Too often those words can mean something completely different to each individual. Our experiences, our relationships, and the circumstances of our lives all filter through the synergy of the senses. The word "senses" itself must be clarified, for it includes more than the common five (vision, hearing, smell, taste, and touch).

There is a *"sixth sense,"* proprioception, a term coined by Sherrington, that gives us a sense or sensation of the body as a whole (Smetacek and Mechsner, 2004). This sixth sense is based on the wholeness of inner sensations in the body, predominantly influenced by the organization of movement patterns. These patterns travel through muscles and bones affecting the mind (more of this will be covered in *Part II of Wellness Through Movement® [WTM®)*. So the proprioceptive sense gives us the capacity to feel the physical sensation behind the state of mind or perception.

How we feel inside dances with what happens "out there" and can be felt as one when we are aware of the physical sensations in the proprioception: this is what I call *Sensory Self-Awareness*. The dance between an internal and external dialogue of sensations (either aware of or blind to the psyche) creates our sense of identity and perception. Being aware of this dance is termed *Sensory Self-Awareness*.

This awareness gives us the option to step out of the dance and watch it. Though calming or centering also happens during the process, the greatest value of this awareness is experiencing the difference between what we are *doing* versus what we *think* we are doing. A passion in the heart, nervousness in the gut, heaviness in the posture all make *physiological commentaries through sensations dialoguing with what we are thinking.* Sensations are the bridge between what we are truly doing and what we want to do.

Sensory Self -Awareness enables our minds to view ourselves from a third perspective

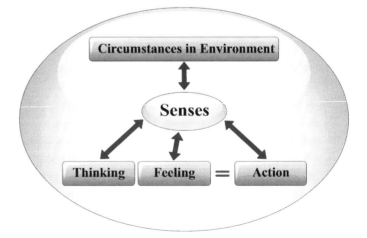

(see the lesson *No Place Like Home Breath)*. In the lesson, the psyche gains the ability to perceive an open landscape, a vision of ourselves from what we called *"Home."* Even in the midst of emotional turbulence, sensory overload, or physical pain and discomfort, there is a sense of centeredness. Children are able to experience this awareness more easily than adults. (See the section on *Notes and Background* under the *Personal Bubbles and No Place Like Home* lesson for more details.)

Acquiring tools to increase Sensory Self-Awareness is now more crucial than ever. One of the leading causes of death for young children between the ages of 10-24 is suicide. Their confusion about the world and about who they are is based on a perception solely directed by what is around them. When "out there" doesn't work, neither do they. Knowing the interconnections among sensory-motor, mental, and emotional reactions is paramount in producing self-reliance, higher academic achievement, and caring and responsible behavior.

Surprisingly, attention turned inside to the sensations of motor patterns connected to perception improves attention and understanding of what is around us. The nature of the nervous system is a two-way street; it correlates the brain and physiological sensations to help us understand concepts. For many, sensory influences of perception are not available to awareness, but if we understand our own perceptual process, we operate more efficiently (Goldstein, 2010; Feldenkrais, 1977). Sensory Self-Awareness inspires innovation and spontaneity. It also motivates self-management, improves social relations, and most important, develops *Emotional Intelligence* (Coleman, 2006).

The purpose of this program is to teach people a kind of self-awareness through the influences of physical sensations. Strategies simultaneously use two tools: attention and movement. *Part I of the Wellness Through Movement®* program teaches strategies combining attention and movement for people to sense more clearly *how the sensations of the body affect the brain.* The intention of the strategies is to increase mindfulness, reduce stress, and help participants become better learners. (See *Appendix A Notes and Background* to learn why and when we do each particular lessons.)

Sensing How We Learn

Sensations play a bigger part in how the mind operates than previously believed, especially for children. "We (especially young people) are feeling creatures that think, not thinking creatures that feel," says neuroanatomist Jill Bolte-Taylor (Bolte-Taylor, 2006). The "sense," often difficult to detect, that correlates thinking, feeling, and acting comes from proprioception. This sixth sense clarifies *how* the mind truly feels and thinks whether this sense is available or not to awareness.

Children are 85% more present in their senses (Hannaford, 2005) than in "logical processing." If we could explain to children a concept of math, reading, or science through sensation, it would be easier for them to learn. In the same way, if children are in touch with their own *Sensory Self-Awareness,* they understand what it means to be "pono," to act in righteousness, and thus they *experience* "pono" from their body to their brain. Because children are bundles of sensations, when their attention is pointed to their bodies, they immediately *recognize* how sensations affect perception and listening. If educated to be self-aware from their bodies to their brains at a young age, the *heart* of perception will direct their choices.

If we ask children to feel their bodies in order to notice their attitude and then ask if the two are associated with each other, they immediately answer yes. Children understand how their bodies influence their brains because they feel it more easily than adults. However, they need to be taught how to pay attention to this connection.

Adult brains have already been conditioned, thus they need to consciously filter out habits of conditioning in order to experience how sensations influence their thoughts.

It seems strange to imagine that our physical sensations can affect our attitudes or moods yet *not* be available to awareness. Many sensations cannot actually be felt without training. Though every square centimeter of the body is full of nerves that provide sensations, as in learning anything, we need time and space to be taught how to operate from center.

The tools used to develop awareness of the association between mind and body are *movement* and *attention.* Movement includes the motion of sensations, breath, and sound (such as in the lesson *Personal Bubbles and No Place Like Home Breath*). When attention is drawn to internal sensations, there is a synergistic effect that expands self-awareness. Internal physical sensations are intermediaries networking information between the self (environment *within* the body) and the immediate surroundings.

Using both tools creates an effect greater than the sum of the whole. If these tools are too subtle for children to use and they cannot shift their perception, further work is needed on a neuromuscular level to re-organize motor patterns. This depth of Sensory Self-Awareness is addressed in *Part II* of *Wellness Through Movement®*.

Adapting the Learner to Academic Curriculum

Elementary teachers introduce a child to the world. Educational science offers ways to train and condition attention to learning from outside of ourselves. Sensory Self-Awareness introduces the person to "who" is the learner. The two directions of teaching – from inside out and outside in - compliment each other. The innate process of how the body/mind learns is based on this two-way road.

Understanding how to integrate Sensory Self-Awareness into academic lessons is explained below; first by a physical lesson, a soccer lesson. Then the same process will be explained in an academic application.

A soccer coach begins a lesson with a task-oriented skill such as handling a ball with feet and then demonstrates how to run with the ball. This demonstration, or modeling, is an "external strategy" of teaching. The player learns not from consciously feeling his/her body, but from seeing and imitating the action of someone else's body.

If a participant is asked, "Where is your attention?" while his/her attention is glued to the coach and the ball, the player's own internal sensations of juggling the ball feel invisible. Teaching how to recognize internal sensations while doing the action with regard to the stimulus adds self-awareness to the task.

Though modeling a skill helps us to learn it, merely imitating haphazardly veils the awareness of internal sensations that could enhance the skill. If attention is directed to the feeling of what we are doing, learning the skill happens easier and quicker.

In a classroom, there is a similar need to pay attention to internal sensations, especially when inaugurating new concepts. For instance, if the lesson is subtraction, some modeling will be useful; but in order to determine the true intention of the lesson (not just rote learning), both teacher and children must embrace the awareness that the brain is actually influenced by the whole self. If the brain is attentive and able to determine how the body is responding to the intended lesson, even when the concept is challenging, the learner becomes more engaged.

If there is confusion or lack of comprehension, the body triggers sensations of tension, heat, and stiffness that fuel emotional frustration and disable learning. Sensations are "wake up calls" to what is happening to thinking before the brain realizes it. Enhancing awareness of sensory acuity (level of sensations) to cognitive thinking is key.

Sensory acuity is the ability to feel differences in weight (heavy or light), brightness, or sound volume, and it is used to measure I.Q. (Gardner, 1999). Sensations recognize a need and are trying to say to the brain: "Hey, wait! I can't think; I can't breathe; I don't understand. I need a break. Maybe I can't think because I can't breathe? Okay, take a deep exhalation and slow down." Bodily sensations and the brain are all part of the same committee, the committee for learning.

When individuals are mindful of their sensations mirroring an emotion, such as anxiety, they have the option of managing these reactions before they get out of hand. The "feeling body" tells the brain what is getting in the way of learning, thus the *whole* person is part of the process of learning the task. What is more, with the guidance of Sensory Self-Awareness, learners understand their personal processes of learning, how attention or distraction is fueled, and what to do in order to relate to the concept being presented. Because the students are recognizing and easing any reactions that might interfere with learning, they take more responsibility for themselves while trying to comprehend the concepts. Students "personalize" the concepts and are thus able to apply them to future challenges and comment on how they feel about the process of learning.

Teacher and Parental Benefits
Improved Communication, Limited Stress, Higher Academic Achievement

Teachers and parents gain benefits from children's Sensory Self-Awareness too. As children learn to manage their stress, identify when they need to take a break or drink water, or use strategies to center themselves, teachers and parents also learn those strategies. Adults become more aware of the tone of voice they use with their children and understand why their children react in ways that are disturbing.

Children become effective communicators, and thus their teachers and parents can better understand how to help them learn. Voicing needs and being part of the learning team come easier to Sensory Self-Aware individuals.

Listening, as opposed to hearing, is related to the degree of one's Sensory Self-Awareness. If children's minds are fully present (aware of symbiotic influences from inside their bodies on what is happening "out there") their ears are fully open to listening. If children are not fully present, they may hear words but not know what is being said. Sensory Self-Awareness then can remind them, from the inside, what has been forgotten. For example, organic urges remind us to relieve the stress level before serious behavioral problems arise. And having fewer behavioral problems changes the evolution of relationships, communication, and academic achievement.

Empathy

Sensory Self-Awareness expands our empathetic reactions to the needs and situations of others. Being able to sense physical reactions depends on the ability to have compassion. This type of compassion (witnessing of sensations) reduces separation between people that may cause hurtful or judgmental opinions. It is easier to be compassionate when we sense the depth of an emotion through a sensation.

When we experience a situation, we understand it better. This "depth and degree" of biological sensations gives a concrete feeling of what is true from the heart of an individual. Such awareness enables an individual to take responsibility in situations of stress or conflict. The more aware we are of ourselves, the easier it is to understand and feel "pono" toward others.

Longer Attention Spans and Self-Directed Learners

Attention span is directly influenced by the amount of internal dialogue that is based on physiological sensations. Sensations "notice" when our energy starts to drain or why our patience and focus begin to scatter long before the "thinking" brain realizes the situation. To be self-directed, we need to be in touch with these subtle sensations that guide our thinking.

Dealing with Reoccurring Challenges and Saving Time

Why does this *new* Sensory Self-Awareness save time? When the organics of our physiological structure sense what we learn, then we remember. Memory is woven into the organic sensation of motor patterns. As the loss of awareness increases and motor patterns become habits, time speeds up - and so does muscle tension. Patterns of sensations remind us of what we have learned. These patterns trap us in habitual reactions if we are not in Sensory Self-Awareness. Sensory Self-Awareness recognizes habits from a neutral perspective. Physical urges in awareness cue us to address needs before the needs become serious challenges.

Sorting and digesting information is quicker and easier when we understand ourselves. "Sorting and digesting" is a psycho-physiological process that will remind us of what we are doing instead of needing constant reminders from teachers and parents.

More time can be focused on curriculum or problem solving when children are in Sensory Self-Awareness. Physical urges from the inside help the children address their behaviors. When Sensory Self-Awareness becomes second nature, self-discovery and learning are engaged. A self-responsible individual is also easier to discipline if intervention is necessary.

Word of caution: Teachers and parents notice that the *No Place Like Home Breath* lesson calms their children, so they use the lesson for that purpose; yet children will get only a temporary benefit from the lesson. It is tempting to use the *Home Breath* to quiet children, but don't overlook the need for Sensory Self-Awareness. Instead of focusing on short-term results, teaching Sensory Self-Awareness through internal physical urges reminds children when to calm and center themselves without needing constant external reminders. When teaching lessons, imagine how the activity can become a lifelong experience for the children. Think about how lessons inspire self-inquiry and self-direction. Rather than leaving it to the teacher or parent to keep children on-task, the "objective" of these lessons is to teach children how to take responsibility for their own actions and attention spans.

Scheduled Movement, Physical Comfort, and Hydration

If children need to move and cannot, a storm of sensations starts brewing inside their minds, and without knowing why, they start being rebellious and arguing with the teacher or parent about the curriculum or situation. Therefore, throughout the daily agenda of studies or activities, teachers and parents should allow for shifts in the physical position of childrens' bodies (and their own bodies) about every 45 minutes or less. We have physiological urges buried beneath habitual patterns that knock on the doors of our minds within this time frame, and the younger the children, the sooner they need to move.

Instead of only doing a movement in the classroom long enough to get the children's focus, remember that they are sense organs. Instead of sedating or disciplining children, how do we help them learn to focus?

Some suggestions: Take a break and roll on the floor, allow individuals to sit or lie in any position as long as they can still listen, and drink water - especially after periods of long-term concentration or if attention is "spacey" from stress. And don't forget to take a bathroom break.

A simple and powerful way to improve mental clarity is to drink water. Drinking water dissolves salts in the body that help the brain cells "talk" to each other. The slightest sense of dehydration, long *before* we feel that cotton sensation in the mouth, reduces the effectiveness of brain function and recall.

Sensory Self-Awareness for Different Ages and Developmental Stages

Knowing *how* to teach Sensory Self-Awareness to children at different ages and developmental stages is essential. The delivery of a lesson must address both the physical conditioning and state of mind of the age group. The younger the child, the shorter but more detailed the guidance needed to sense movement. Looking for specific clues to sense the body clearly, such as *how* the body is touching the floor and where it is difficult to feel the body, can become a mystery game (see *Pancake Body* lesson). Learning through the context of games makes it easier for young children to understand the value of the lesson. The *Notes and Background* section goes into more detail about how each game offers a lesson in Sensory Self-Awareness.

If children learn in positive situations, they will be self-directed in choosing tools for centering when they are upset. This is the main reason why movement games are used to teach attention and help children experience how to look inside to discover physical sensations that affect thinking.

Sensory Self-Awareness games are cumulative. If done in the recommended sequential order, an organic intelligence will take over and continue the teaching; this organic intelligence is the source of innovation. Though there may be need for reminders to "sense" the body, having this kind of creative "fun" makes learning easier and encourages self-directed learners long after the lesson is done.

Sensory Self-Awareness for Health and Obesity

Obesity is a growing problem in America, especially for children. If training in *Sensory Self-Awareness* starts at a young age, healthier food choices will be easier to make and knowing how much food to eat will be based on physical urges. Sometimes our heads want more food, but our stomachs are full.

Once children learn to recognize sensations available through Sensory Self-Awareness, they can also distinguish differences in what the sensations are trying to tell them such as: the need for food, the need for water, or sluggishness caused by eating foods that do not agree with their metabolisms. Foods can also change moods and contribute to depression if an individual has biological sensitivities (Shenkin, Schachter, and Hutton, 1987).

Sensations are constantly trying to take care of us. When we are aware of these sensations, they help to adjust our posture before we are drained, improve our breathing before we feel light-headed, and even let us know when to take a break. Thousands of other physiological urges from this *internal physician of sensations* demand the expansion of Sensory Self-Awareness.

Sensory Self-Awareness is not something made up; it is the nature of how our nervous system is designed.

Summary

The capacity to understand our intentions, motivations, and desires starts with the capacity to understand ourselves. For the mind to develop a neutral mode of perspective, the brain must inquire and reflect on the integration of the whole self: mind, body, and heart.

Self-awareness is different for everyone; each unique "organic self" determines how different. These differences in perception are created by differences in the quality of sensations. No two people have the same body, metabolism, or perception. The internal dialogue of perception differs according to the functional integration of sensations. How we *experience* a situation is different for each of us, just as how we reason is different. The functioning of mind, body, sensation, and reasoning are inseparable.

The greatest gift of bodily sensations is that they teach us awareness of the self. The senses biologically steer us into patterns to bring us into awareness. Sensations mirror all the processes of the mind, but also "know" where to find balance when in awareness. Sensations mirror "what is" to wake up awareness of what we are doing: they do not say one thing is good and another is bad, be it emotional, intellectual, or physical. In Sensory Self-Awareness, we step back and sense the interconnections between mind and body without being swallowed up by the sensations.

To maintain self-reflectiveness, even amidst turbulent emotions, we must find a non-judgmental perception in a world full of judgments. This innocent mind, similar to the non-judgmental mind of a toddler, has the wisdom of what "makes sense." We need to remember that this innocent mind is always there beneath any turbulence, and perceive through those eyes. The physiological wisdom our minds receive through sensations is tangible feedback we cannot deny.

Despite our differences, we share one common thread: the organic synergy of the body and the heart. We need structure to develop cognitive reasoning, but we also need to know ourselves. Teaching children to understand **how they think** is inseparable from **what they think**. When we "feel," we understand. Our physiology provides the mind with the means *to find* a neutral observer of our mental, emotional, and physical processes.

Self-direction from integration of mind, body, and heart produces quality choices for humanity; "complex thinkers" can then address multiple challenges from an innovative perspective. What is more, Sensory Self-Awareness will inspire people to be more effective communicators and to be more responsible for their health, education, work, and home life.

Attention inside clarifies attention outside. We know this intuitively and personally, and we are starting to prove it scientifically; living it will change each individual and the world. To inspire children and to value "who" they are completely, we must learn attention from the *inside out*. If we did, **we would all be sensational.**

The goal of the program is to make *New* Sensory *Self-Awareness* a lifestyle. Learning Sensory Self-Awareness is what the innate intelligence of the nervous system is trying to show us. The experience of *Sensory Self-Awareness* gives the mind a kind of love that is neutral, humble, and openhearted –a mode of perception to use with others and with ourselves.

GETTING STARTED

Prepare for a Lesson

The following two steps are essential to <u>all</u> the lessons and must be used to start every session.

Start with the Muscle-Testing lesson to check hydration; help participants learn how to take care of themselves first by being able to sense subtle sensations like the need for water.
Be sure to provide water in the classroom, and start every lesson by asking the participants to notice if they feel thirsty.

Hydration
Ask them to remember how it feels to be thirsty and encourage them to drink water when they need it throughout the day, both at home and at school.

Why is drinking water so important before a lesson?
> Water helps dissolve the salts in the body. When these salts dissolve, an ionic charge helps the synapses (one nerve cell to another) communicate. Communication from one part of the body to the other is dependent on this electrical impulse transaction. When the muscles sense how all parts are related to one another, health and learning improve in both the body and brain.

Reflection
Taking time to reflect on sensations <u>before, during, and after</u> each lesson is crucial. For instance, just drinking water before each lesson without considering how each participant feels would lessen conscious awareness of physical sensations. Reflecting on earlier lessons before starting the next lesson enables the participants to draw on earlier sensations and to become more aware of new sensations as they are practiced. Using questions to draw attention to how sensations differ before the lesson versus afterward is recommended.

Foundational to all the lessons
Recommended: Please start with *Personal Bubbles Freeze Dance.* This lesson introduces the other important lesson: *Personal Bubbles and No Place Like Home Breath.*
   o   This lesson is foundational for all three parts of the *Wellness Through Movement®* program because it is about the heart. The "heart" in this book refers to a sense of centeredness, mindfulness, and wholeness. Brain and heart researchers at the Institute of HeartMath reported: "The heart's electromagnetic field is by far the most powerful produced by the body; it's approximately 5000 times greater in strength than the fields produced by the brain. It can be measured up to 8-10 feet away with sensitive detectors called magnetometers" (Childre and Martin, 1999, p. 33). The combinations of these two lessons mentioned above are keys to enhancing the proprioceptive sense (body orientation and synergy of the senses giving perception), which is the foundation of all learning.

Muscle-Testing for Water

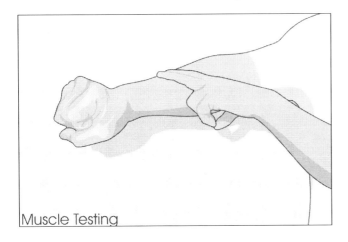

Muscle Testing

GO!

Begin Muscle Testing for Water

1. Ask participants if they need water.

2. Ask participants to line up and put one arm perpendicular to their bodies, straight elbow, making a fist, and "be strong."

3. While they are strong, ask them if they need water.

4. Push down gently but firmly on their forearm:
    If movement is jumpy or weak, they need water.
    If you have difficulty measuring differences, try this:
        Ask participants to repeat this statement: "My name is _____ ."
        Note the level of strength in their arm.
        Then repeat the statement, but have them make up a name.
        Test again and have them notice the difference in the strength.

5. Repeat arm testing after drinking lots of water.

CLOSING

Reflection:
o   Ask participants how they feel at the end compared to the beginning of the lesson! What is different?

OBJECTIVE

To get the children curious about their bodies and how muscles can affect thinking or being thirsty

To help children learn how to take care of themselves; first, by being able to sense subtle sensations like the need for water

PREPARE

o   Read Appendix A *Notes and Background* to understand the purpose and how to do the lesson
o   Equipment: Drinking water
o   **Reflect** : Ask participants to notice how they feel sitting at their desks before and after the lesson

LESSON SEQUENCES

Lessons are cumulative. Enjoy the journey!

Level 1   Foundational Lessons
Level 2   Core Lessons
Level 3   All Ages
Level 4   Adults

LEVEL 1 FOUNDATIONAL LESSONS

Personal Bubbles Freeze Dance

No Place Like Home Breath

LEVEL 2 CORE LESSONS

Pancake Body

Personal Bubbles Freeze Dance

Personal Bubbles & No Place Like Home Breath

Big Tiny Bubbles

No Place Like Home Breath

LEVEL 3 ALL AGES

Pancake Body

↓

Personal Bubbles Freeze Dance

↓

Personal Bubbles & No Place Like Home Breath

↓

Big Tiny Bubbles

↓

No Place Like Home Breath

↓

Body Bubbles

↓

Listening Bubbles

↓

Over, Under, Around

↓

Hokey Pokey Body Bubble

↓

Ho'oponopono Home

For 3rd, 4th, or 5th grades replace
Personal Bubbles Freeze Dance
with
Hula Relay Personal Bubbles or
Dancin' Hula Hoops

LEVEL 4 ADULTS

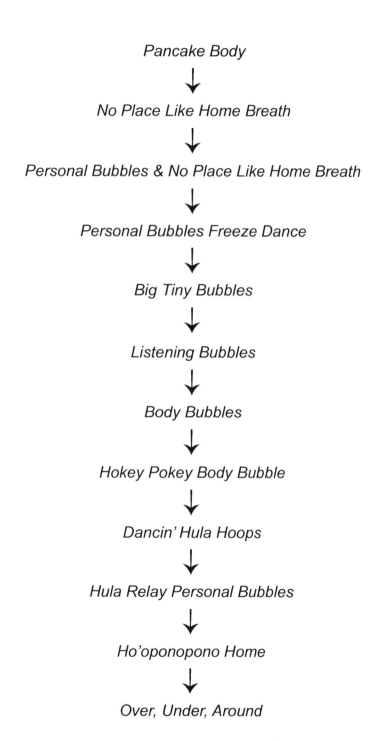

Pancake Body

↓

No Place Like Home Breath

↓

Personal Bubbles & No Place Like Home Breath

↓

Personal Bubbles Freeze Dance

↓

Big Tiny Bubbles

↓

Listening Bubbles

↓

Body Bubbles

↓

Hokey Pokey Body Bubble

↓

Dancin' Hula Hoops

↓

Hula Relay Personal Bubbles

↓

Ho'oponopono Home

↓

Over, Under, Around

PART I LESSONS

Lessons are cumulative, organically building awareness to have a direct experience of how sensations influence thoughts.

Pancake Body

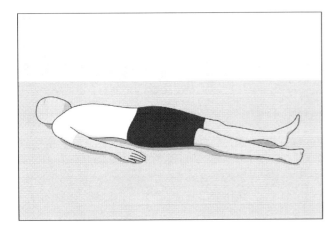

OBJECTIVES

Become aware of the body's position and organization in relation to attitude

Improve awareness of the connections between physical sensations and thinking

Become aware of spatial orientation inside the body

Introduce the internal influence of external factors: pressure, weight, and space

PREPARE

o   **Review Appendix A *Notes and Background*** to understand the purpose and how to deliver the lesson.

o   **Clear and clean** floor space.

o   **Hydrate** (See *Getting Started* page 33). If participants are really energetic, have them run in place as fast and as long as possible. If applicable, ask: What do you remember from the last time we met to rekindle memory and the physical sensation to memory?

o   **Recommendation:** Do this lesson at the beginning and ending of a day or lesson.

GO !

Begin Pancake Body
1. Lie on back with arms and legs straight and at rest on floor.

2. Notice how the arms, legs, and back are touching or only partly touching the floor.

3. For young participants ask:
   "Where could a mongoose run underneath your pancake body?"
   "How tall is the mongoose that can run under your neck, waist, knees, etc."

4. For older children or adults suggest:
   "Feel the 5 lines of the body (spine, both legs, and arms) and position of skull."

5. "Feel where the line of right arm is touching the floor, what parts of the arm feel heavy, and what part is not touching."
   o Continue with the line of the right leg, both the right arm and right leg, and then the whole right side of the body.

6. Repeat steps in #5 with the left side of the body.
   Ask: "Are the arms and legs on right/left sides the same or different?"

CLOSING

Reflection
   o Key to this lesson is to do *Pancake Body* at the beginning and ending of the lesson or day. Then compare the "echo" of sensation (the change in muscle sensation to attitude) from the beginning to the end of the lesson or day.

   o Ask: "Did the mongoose (space under the body) change sizes after the lesson?" "Did the floor get softer after the lesson? How?"

Personal Bubbles Freeze Dance

OBJECTIVES

To narrow conditioned attention from "out there" to "inside"

To feel the inner and outer world simultaneously

To develop participants' ability to change what is perceived around them

To build self-respect and respect for others

To build spatial awareness and trust with others

PREPARE

o **Review Appendix A** *Notes and Background* to understand the purpose and how to deliver the lesson.

o **Equipment**: Cones and hula hoops for half of the class, sheer, colorful veils (for 3- 6 year olds). Clock with second hand or stopwatch, and/or music and boom box. (Suggestion: *Where is the Love* and *Let's Get Started* by Black Eyed Peas.)

o **Clear and clean** floor (or outdoor) space and set up cones to mark a clear, rectangular boundary line.

o **Hydrate** (See *Getting Started*). Recommended: Begin and end with *Pancake Body (page 40)*. Review *Personal Bubbles and Home Breath* Lesson.

o **During Lesson Assess** how participants use personal space by watching dynamics of (physical and emotional) interactions.

o **Demonstrate Finding Bubble:** Pick a volunteer. Sit face-to-face and slowly lean in toward the volunteer's face until he/she reacts by blinking, changing rhythm of breath, giggling, or moving in any other way. Point out that you just touched the volunteer's *Personal Bubble*. Have participants try this in pairs. Ask participants to NOTICE differences in personal bubble sizes.

o **Difficulty in finding bubble:** Ask the group to help by having them watch the face of the volunteer as demonstrator leans in toward the volunteer's face.

GO!

Begin Personal Bubble Freeze Dance - *two or three rounds as time allows.* Like *TAG* with everyone "it," but no one can touch another.

Round One:
1. Start music and say, "Go" (or start stop watch)
2. Participants begin to move; if they bump into each other, the music stops and everyone "freeze."
3. Everyone must find his or her *Personal Bubble* again. Remind participants of how they originally found their personal bubble and how big that space was. Help participants to NOTICE how long they played without popping bubbles and whether they respected each other.
4. Start the music again and repeat the exercise two or three times or until no one bumps into anyone else.
5. Ask participants how they began to respect their own space and that of others.

Round Two:
1. Ask participants to see how long they can keep the music playing (see if the time lengthens from the start to the end of the round.)
2. Increase the challenge with more hula hoops on ground at narrow boundaries:
   o Place hula hoops on ground as imaginary holes. Participants must not touch each other's bubbles or hoops (hopping over hoops is acceptable without bumping).
3. If bumping is frequent, reduce the challenge by following one of the following strategies:
   o Give young children sheer, colorful veils to represent their personal bubbles.
   o Give participants their own "personal space" near a cone or outside boundary where they can run in place (helps to relieve extra energy).
   o Repeat exercise several times without the hoops.
4. When participants have stayed within their "own personal space," ask them if the music played longer this time.

Round Three: If time allows, review the (*No Place Like*) *Home Breath* lesson if necessary (page 46). Do *Home Breath* lesson to help participants find their centers in relation to others.
1. Start music and continue with *Personal Bubbles Freeze Dance* while remembering the feeling of "*Home*" inside, even with eyes open.
2. Important: Help participants to notice how to feel "*Home*" inside while playing the game and to notice how many fewer bumps there are.

CLOSING

Reflection:
o Ask the whole group to share their experiences when their bubbles are popped.
o Ask the participants how they felt before and after the game and how they can use this game to help them in school, at work, or at home.
o Ask if the participants are aware of the importance of respecting others and themselves.
o Ask the participants to notice how they can use the *Home Breath* lesson in life as they do in the *Personal Bubbles Freeze Dance* (to be aware in conflicted, stressful, or anxious times).

Personal Bubbles &
No Place Like Home Breath
(Also Known as Pono Breath)

OBJECTIVES

Personal Bubbles:
Develop self-awareness through sensations *from* body to mind

Develop compassion, trust, and respect for self and others

No Place Like Home Breath:
Become aware of the feeling of *Home* inside the body and how it influences the mind

Foster the ability to change perception through physical sensations

Learn breathing strategies to center mind and body

PREPARE

o   **Review Appendix A *Notes and Background*** to understand the purpose and how to deliver the lesson.

o   **Hydrate** (See *Getting Started*)

o   **Recommendation:** Do *Personal Bubble Freeze Dance* lesson (page 42) before this lesson: Ask participants what they remember from this lesson.

o   **Prepare** space where participants can sit and face one another in pairs. If participants are really energetic, have them run in place as fast and as long as possible.

o   Teachers: Please experience the breathing technique to better understand the effects.

GO!

Begin Personal Bubbles (Space <u>around</u> the body versus inside as in *Body Bubbles* lesson)
    1.   Have participants face each other in pairs, and have one person slowly lean toward his or her partner's face until the partner reacts by blinking, giggling, or breathing differently. Remind the person that he or she has entered the partner's *Personal Bubble.*

2. Have the person's partner repeat the exercise, noticing the first person's reaction when he or she enters the partner's *Personal Bubble.*

3. Reflection: Ask the participants to notice the differences in each person's *Personal Bubble.*

Begin No Place Like Home Breath (Space <u>inside</u> the body). *For young* participants *discuss: "This is a different "Home" than the one we live in. It is <u>inside</u> our bodies."*

1. Reflection: Ask the participants to notice how they are feeling (tired, anxious, calm).

2. Have participants sit comfortably (with crossed legs) or have them lie on their backs. If they are very energetic or excited, have them lie on their bellies with knees bent and feet in the air, resting their heads on the floor and gently rocking their legs right and left. (Being on belly is a good position for hyperactive young children.)

3. Inhale deeply and PAUSE while holding the deep breath.

4. Exhale gently and at length while softly humming the sound "Hommmmmmme."
(If lying on belly, gently rock legs left and right.) Repeat 2 to 4 times. (Young children should REST rather than PAUSE, to avoid hyperventilation.)

5. To deepen participants' awareness with the sensation of *"Home,"* ask each person to notice where he or she feels the vibration while humming. Have them put their hands on their bodies where they feel the vibration end. Encourage them to notice the feeling in their whole body at the end of the exhalation. This feeling inside is referred to as *"Home."*

6. Repeat the process (3 times for younger children; up to 12 times for older children or adults). Repeat inhalation and exhalation with eyes open and then with eyes closed. Ask participants which way makes it easier to feel *"Home."*

CLOSING

Reflection:
○ Ask the participants: "How did you feel at the start of the lesson? How did you feel after doing the *Home Breath*? What is different in your mind or body?"
○ Ask the participants if they feel different after doing *No Place Like Home Breath.* "How could you use *No Place Like Home Breath* to help you? How could you use these exercises at school or at home? When do we need to center ourselves?"
○ Ask the participants: "Can you feel *"Home"* *inside* of your *Personal Bubble?*"
○ Suggestion: "Imagine a stressful situation. Try doing the *Home Breath* and remember the feeling of *"Home."* Now let *"Home"* speak. Notice if perception and how we speak changes while addressing the stressful situation.

No Place Like Home Breath

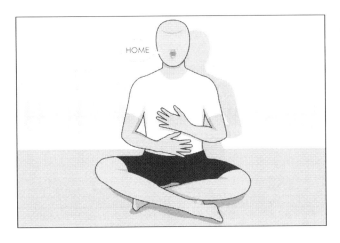

OBJECTIVES

Learn how breathing strategies center the mind and body

Become aware of interior sensations during inhalations and exhalations

Become aware of the feeling of "*Home*" inside the body and mind

Build spatial awareness and trust with self and others

PREPARE

○ **Review Appendix A *Notes and Background*** to understand the purpose and how to deliver the lesson.

○ Teachers: Please do the breathing technique with the participants in order to better understand the breathing process.

○ **Hydrate** (See *Getting Started page 33*)

○ If participants are really energetic, have them run in place *quickly* for as long as possible.

GO!

Begin No Place Like Home Breath

For young children, discuss: This is a different <u>"Home"</u> than the one we live in. It is <u>inside</u> our bodies.

1. Sit (cross-legged), lie on back or lie on belly with knees bent and feet in air, head resting on the ground (being on belly is a good position for hyperactive young children).

2. Inhale deeply and pause while holding a deep breath.

3. Exhale gently and at length while humming quietly the word *"Hommmmmmmmmme."* (If lying on belly, gently rock legs left and right)

4. Pause at the end of each exhalation. Repeat three to five times then notice the feeling of *"Home"* in *attitude* and *physical sensation*. This feeling is called *"Home."*

5. To deepen the awareness of "being calm," ask participants to put a hand on their body where the exhalation ends (each place may be different)

6. Repeat inhalation and exhalation with eyes open and then with eyes closed. Ask participants which way makes it easier to feel *"Home?"*

CLOSING

Reflection:

o Ask the participants: "What is the difference in our attitude and physical feeling when we have attention towards *"Home?"* "How did you feel before doing *Home Breath* and after doing *Home Breath?"*

o Ask participants: "How could you use *Home Breath* to help you? When do we need to calm ourselves?"

o Suggest: Imagine a stressful situation. Try doing a *Home Breath* and notice if you feel differently, or perception changes, towards the situation.

Big Tiny Bubbles

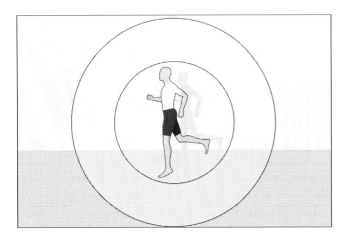

OBJECTIVES

To develop more spatial awareness within the body in relationship with others and the environment

To build respect for others

PREPARE

○ **Review Appendix A *Notes and Background* t**o understand the purpose and how to deliver the lesson.

○ **Equipment**: Boom box or iPod for music (see *Notes and Background, Appendix A* for suggestions), clock with second hand or stopwatch, cones (optional: hula hoops).

○ **Set up boundary line** for movement area. The size depends on the number of participants. For 20 students, set up a 25 x 30 foot area (smaller area is more challenging).

○ **Optional**: Create different boundary shapes on the floor with cones (if outside) or tape (indoors). Make triangles, squares, circles, or diamonds or use hula hoops as directed below to create areas that are off limits during the game.

○ **Hydrate** (Review *Getting Started page 33*).

○ **Explain the object of the game** (review *Personal Bubbles Freeze Dance page 42*): While the music plays, the participants move around the shaped areas without bumping others. If they bump another participant, they have popped their *Personal Bubble* and the music or timer will stop while they freeze. (If participants are hyperactive, have them run in place outside the boundaries or do *Home Breath*. Review *Personal Bubbles No Place Like Home Breath*). When they are calm, resume the game.

GO!

Begin Big Tiny Bubbles

1. Play music and/or start timer. See how long participants can move within boundaries without touching each other or shapes on ground.
2. After two touches, stop the game and reflect back to the feeling of *"Home" (see No Place Like Home Breath page 46)*.
3. Repeat, but this time imagine BIG bubbles around participants' bodies (they will be farther away from each other as a result). Time the game and see how long the participants can go without bumping. *Optional:* Participants can hold hula hoops around them to define their bubbles.
4. Repeat again, however each participant imagines a TINY bubble around the body. Encourage the participants to come as close as possible to each other without touching. Stop and start the music or timer several times. Share with participants the importance of noticing how they feel when others come close.
5. Note the changes in times of how long participants played without bumping and discuss why the times are different. *Optional*: Increase the challenge by placing hula hoops on the floor and instruct participants to avoid touching each other or the hula hoops. They can hop over the hula hoops only if they do not touch one another.

CLOSING

Reflection:

o   Repeat the beginning of the lesson by going back to imagining BIG bubbles with music and timer.

o   Ask: Did the amount of time change between the first timed game and the last one? Why do they think that the time changed? How is Big Tiny Bubbles related to respect? (Hint: awareness of physical space is a sensation that helps memory and spatial orientation.)

o   Ask: How can we increase awareness and respect for each other with awareness of our own and others' bubbles? Will this awareness be helpful at home, school, work, or play?

Listening Bubbles

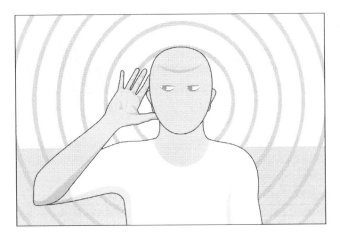

OBJECTIVES

Build awareness of why we do or do not listen (how we hear our own thoughts more clearly than exterior words or sounds)

Improve respect for others

Introduce the concept of the physical space occupied by sound (based on how far away we can hear loud or soft sounds)

PREPARE

o **Review Appendix A *Notes and Background*** to understand the purpose and how to deliver the lesson.

o **Hydrate** (See *Getting Started* page 33).

o **Recommendation**: Participants must do *Personal Bubbles and Home Breath* lessons (page 44) to give them a sense of how the physical space in the body is associated with the physical space where sound travels.

GO!

Begin Listening Bubbles: Outer Sound

1. Tell participants that *Personal Bubbles* are also involved in listening. Example: Talk in a whisper so faint that the participants will need to come just a few inches from you in order to hear you (like listening to a whispered secret).

2. When they are close, ask them if your *Listening Bubble* is big or small. Why is it small?

3. Repeat the exercise; this time ask participants to move away from your soft whisper (or louder voice) until they can/cannot hear you (get outside of your *Listening Bubble*).

4. Ask: How big is the *Listening Bubble* now?

5. Ask: How can we "pop" *Listening Bubbles*? Answer: When someone is speaking and we speak or make noise at the same time.

Begin Listening Bubbles: Inner Sound (sound inside our minds so that we have no attention or are not listening)

1. Move close to a person who is busy doing something else and not listening (or attending).
2. Ask participants to notice that *Listening Bubbles* can disappear even if we are right next to a person. (If participants laugh at the person not listening, remind them that they have "popped" the *Listening Bubble* by not staying in their "*Home*" inside.)
3. <u>Key Message to convey</u>: Even though we have ears, sometimes we cannot hear because we are listening only to our minds.

CLOSING

Reflection:

o Relate the above experiences to respect for each other's *Listening Bubbles*.
o Relate respect in listening to respect of physical space in *Personal Bubbles*.
o Ask: How can we use *Listening* or *Personal Bubbles* (in school, during free time, or at home)?
o Help participants understand when they are not listening due to the internal commentary of their own *feelings*.
o Help participants associate the *feeling* of how different they are with themselves and each other when remembering *Listening Bubbles*.
o Point out that there are *Listening Bubbles* and *Personal Bubbles* in all situations.
o Ask: How do *Listening Bubbles* and *Personal Bubbles* make it easier to share time and space with others?

Body Bubbles

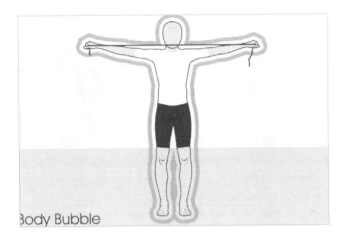

Body Bubble

OBJECTIVES

To expand awareness of the space inside the body (orientation within the body or proprioceptive sense, space around the body, and the 19 senses)

To increase spatial awareness around the body

To Increase spatial awareness with others

PREPARE

o **Review Appendix A *Notes and Background*** to understand the purpose and how to deliver the lesson.

o **Equipment**: boom box, hula hoops, large roll of colorful string or yarn, (optional for very young children: 3' x 3' sheer scarves).

o **Set up boundary line** for movement area. The size depends on the number of participants. For 20 participants, set up a 25 x 30 foot area (smaller area is more challenging).

o **Do *Pancake Body*** (page 40) or ask participants to lie on the floor and notice how big their bodies feel, how long, how tall, how heavy or light.

o **Hydrate** (See *Getting Started*). Review *Personal Bubbles Home Breath* lesson.

GO!

Begin Body Bubbles
o Part I (Similar to *Personal Bubble Freeze Dance*)
  1. Ask participants to remember the feeling of their personal bubbles. If you did <u>not</u> do *Personal Bubbles*, ask participants to imagine a big bubble around themselves. (In this situation it is okay to demonstrate a big bubble between people.)
  2. Start moving with the music; if a participant touches another, the bubble "pops" and the music stops.
  3. When the music stops, everyone must "freeze." (Anyone who does not freeze must step

outside the boundary and run in place until he/she is more relaxed and feels ready to rejoin the game.)

4. Repeat: Music starts and participants start moving inside their personal bubbles.

5. Ask: "How long can we keep the music going?" The length of time the music plays without anyone's bubble popping shows them how well bubbles are respected.

6. Options to increase the challenge:
    a. Two participants get within one hula hoop without touching each other; then, they move around together
    b. Place hula hoops on the ground to represent "holes." Participants must "freeze" if they touch or enter the hula-hoop interior.

7. *Optional* to help very young participants feel their personal bubbles: Ask them to place the sheer scarves over their heads and then "freeze" if they touch another's scarf/bubble.

- Part II
    1. Finding *Body Bubbles* (space *inside* the body). Gather participants together. Ask: "Do you think your arm span is as long as your whole body?"
    2. Cut string or yarn to measure arm span (fingertips to fingertips with arms outstretched to sides).
    3. Compare cut string to each participant's height. (Note: string represents the size of the "body bubble"). Ask: "Can you find your *'Home'* inside your body bubble?" (Review Lesson 4 *No Place Like Home Breath* page 46 if necessary.)
    4. Participants should touch body bubble with one hand on top of their heads and put the other hand on the back of their heads.
        a. Now ask participants to *feel* the body bubble of their heads in between their hands. (Hint: Feel space between hands.)
        b. Repeat touching from front to back or from side to side other parts of the body in order to notice how they <u>feel their *"Home"*</u> (see *Home Breath* lesson) inside the body bubble.

CLOSING

Reflection:

- Repeat *Body Bubbles* freeze game again. Ask whether participants notice if the music played longer when personal bubbles are not "popped."

- End by having all participants resting on floor as they did at the start of the lesson. Ask: "Do you notice if your body feels different now than at the start of the lesson?" or "Do you feel more aware of your personal bubble?"

- Suggestion: Allow the participants to take their strings that measured arm-spans home to share with their families.

Hokey Pokey Body Bubble

OBJECTIVES

Clarify the sense of body in space

Improve sense of balance

Increase listening skills

Increase self awareness of the whole body by organizing movement of body parts

Build vocabulary of body parts (just "right" and "left" for young children).

PREPARE

o **Review Appendix A *Notes and Background*** to understand the purpose and how to deliver the lesson.

o **Hydrate** (See *Getting Started.*) If applicable, ask: What do you remember from the last time we met?

GO!

Begin Hokey Pokey Body Bubble

1. Rest on back and feel both sides of body; remember that feeling to compare at end of lesson

2. Start singing the Hokey Pokey

3. <u>Starting sequence</u>: (attention directs the nature of how the nervous system senses the body in space, the body between its parts, and which parts are functioning)

4. "You put your <u>whole body</u> in/out"... then:

5. <u>Right</u> side first (lower body):
   Put your whole right side in/out
   Put your right foot in/out (grounding function)
   Put your right knee in/out (locomotion function)
   Put your right hip in/out (directional function)

6. <u>Right</u> side first (upper body)

Put your right hand in/out (sense the relationship of hand to "out"side the body)
Put your right elbow in/out (sense of self-direction function)
Put your right shoulder in/out (outer directional function)

7. Left side of head (neural control of organs in the skull switches to the opposite side)
Put your left ear "in/out" (sense of lateral orientation and balance)
Put your right eye "in/out" (relationship (window) to the world with heart connection)

Rest: Briefly, if there is time, lie on back before continuing on left side

8. Left side (lower body)
Put your whole left side in/out
Put your left foot in/out (grounding function)
Put your left knee in/out (locomotion function)
Put your left hip in/out (directional function)

9. Left side (upper body)
Put your left hand in/out (external relationship function)
Put your left elbow in/out (self-directional function)
Put your left shoulder in/out (external/internal relationship)

10. Right side head (neural control of organs in the head switch to the opposite side)
Put your left ear "in/out" (lateral balance function)
Put your left eye "in/out" (window to the world, heart connection)

11. Left side (of whole body)

12. For head reverse: Left side of head followed by right side of body

13. Put your whole front in/out (sense directional differentiation)
Put your whole body in/out (sense differences in body from beginning to end of the dance)

14. Rest. Adults: Rest on back, then walk for 15-20 minutes. Children: Rest on back to feel differences and/or use 10 minutes of free time for walking, running.

CLOSING

Reflection:
○ Hydrate again.
○ Ask how the participants feel now as opposed to how they felt before starting the dance. How do they feel after completing the dance on both sides of the body versus how they felt during the first rest period?

Dancin' Hula Hoops

OBJECTIVES

To increase spatial awareness within and around the body

To improve awareness of the body core and soften the spiral movement of rotation in the spine

To improve posture

PREPARE

o **Review Appendix A Notes and Background** to understand the purpose and how to deliver the lesson.

o **Recommendation:** Do lessons *No Place Like Home* and *Listening Bubbles* before this lesson.

o **Hydrate** (See *Getting Started page 33*)

o **Equipment**: Two to four hula hoops per child.

o **Set up** a large boundary. The size of boundary depends on the number of participants and their level of spatial awareness. Intention is to establish awareness of movement in a structured boundary. *Recommended:* Review *Personal Bubbles* and *Home Breath* lessons before this lesson, especially if working with young children.

o **Ask** participants to notice and remember where in the room they are sitting (cross legged on floor) and in which direction they are facing so they can return at the end of the lesson to the <u>exact position</u> (of their body *and* their orientation to the room) they faced at the start. This will enable them to accurately compare subtle differences at the end of the lesson. Then ask them to twist, looking right and left (without moving knees), what they see when they twist, and how their bodies feel as they twist.

GO!

Begin Dancin' Hula-Hoops

1. Participants each get a hula hoop and begin to use it, being careful to respect each others' *Personal Bubbles (*see *Personal Bubbles Freeze Dance* lesson for reference page 42*)*.
2. Continue to use hula hoops, and while maintaining their *Personal Bubbles,* have participants begin to walk, then run, walk sideways, and walk backwards.
3. *To Increase the challenge:* When participants master one hula hoop, use two hula hoops.
4. Increase challenge again, once by adding more hula hoops, or by using the hula hoop on one ankle while moving across the ground. Then use the opposite ankle and notice if one ankle is easier than the other - or if they feel different.

CLOSING

Reflection:

o   Return to the start of the lesson, sitting cross-legged, and twist right and then left.
o   Ask: Are you sitting in exactly the same position as at the start and looking in the same direction? Do you feel the same now when you twist as you did at the start? Does your back feel the same or different? Is it easier now to notice your surroundings or to pay attention? How can we apply what we noticed in this lesson in our lives at home or at school?

Hula Relay Personal Bubbles

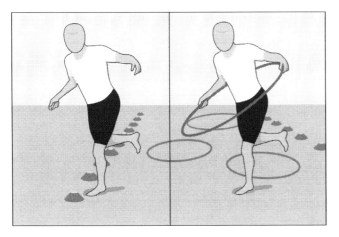

OBJECTIVES

Feel "inside" and "out there" simultaneously

Improve spatial awareness within and around the body

Develop awareness and respect for others

Integrate spiral rotation, agility, and balance with centeredness

PREPARE

○ **Review Appendix A** *Notes and Background* to understand the purpose and how to deliver the lesson.

○ **Recommendation:** Do *Personal Bubbles and No Place Like Home Breath* lesson to improve listening skills in this game.

○ **Hydrate** (See *Getting Started page 33*).

○ **Equipment**: Hula hoops (8 of same color per team), cones, and placement markers.

○ **Set up an obstacle course** of cones and hula hoops (see diagram above). If there are multiple teams, set up the course using a different color for each team.

○ **Space hula hoops** in an alternating diagonal line-up (see diagram above). Place cones to form one large boundary for all line-ups. Space team lanes about one foot apart.

○ **Divide participants into teams** (three to eight students per team). Assign a color to each team, and ask each team to line up in front of their team-colored hula hoops.

GO!

Begin Hula Relay Personal Bubbles

1. Begin without holding a hula hoop; participants must run *around* the outside of the hula hoops (the first round they are allowed to hop over them) in their own team's lane, going down the row and back to the starting line **without bumping into members of the other teams**. When one participant completes the row and returns, he or she tags the next team member and then sits at the back of the team line (walk pre-school children through the task if necessary.)

2. *Optional, but recommended:* If the runner touches a hoop or bumps a member of another team, he or she must forfeit the turn or return to the end of the line and do a *Home Breath* to calm down before trying again.

3. Repeat the game, but this time, for more exercise and to fuel excitement, the participant returns to the start of the course, and he or she should run straight back to the starting line as fast as possible.

4. To increase the challenge, each participant now carries a hula hoop - as in illustration above. The whole team runs through the course; but this time without touching hoops on the ground or held by participants.

5. Addition lesson options: If you have a stopwatch, *add up* team or individual times. Add all the team times for the first relay and compare with added scores from the second relay.

6. Multiplication or division lesson options: Multiply one team's score by another team's score. Practice division by determining how many participants will be on each team (24 children on 3 teams = 8 per team; 24 on 4 teams = 6, etc.).

CLOSING

Reflection:
- While children drink water, ask them to NOTICE what the game has demonstrated.
- Ask: What has the game taught about playing at recess? Why are math lessons important for us to learn? How could we respect another's personal space at home? Do we feel different from before to after the game? How?

Ho'oponopono Home 1*

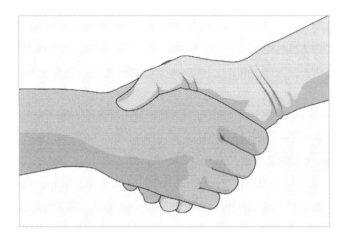

OBJECTIVES

Improve communication skills

Improve social skills and relationships

Build respect for self and others

Learn conflict resolution skills by speaking whole truth, from the heart, not the head

PREPARE

- ○ **Review Appendix A Notes and Background** to understand the purpose and how to deliver the lesson.

- ○ **Hydrate** (See *Getting Started*) and review *No Place Like Home Breath*.

- ○ **Watch** for conflicts during class or free time.

- ○ **Ask** those in the conflict to join you in a circle. (Release others to work, free time or lunch as appropriate in order to ensure privacy.)

GO!

Begin Ho'oponopono Home 1

- o Introduce *Ho'oponopono Home* as a communication tool for conflict resolution.

- o Procedure for *Ho'oponopono Home*:

  1. Sit in the circle with participants in conflict. Ask participants to go into *"Home"* (See *No Place Like Home Breath* page 46). The person with most emotional charge talks first while everyone else listens.

  2. Make it clear that each individual has valuable opinions and will get a turn to talk. The second person in the conflict repeats to the first speaker what he/she understood the first speaker to say (in a <u>compassionate</u> and polite manner) until the first speaker feels "heard."

  3. Then the second person shares his/her version of what happened and the first person listens and then (<u>compassionately</u>) recounts that message.

  4. Ask the other participants in the circle to come up with a possible solution without taking sides.

  5. Ask the participants in controversy: "How can you be friends again? Can you shake hands?" Be sure they are looking into each other's eyes. If they look away, ask compassionately if they can respect the other person by looking at them while they speak.

CLOSING

Reflection:

- o Ask all children in the group if they think this process will help them in both school and free time.

- o Congratulate them all for their good work.

*There is a *Ho'oponopono Home I* and *II* (see *Part II*).

Over, Under, Around

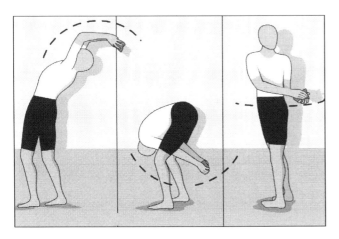

OBJECTIVES

Attention to the physical sensation of an action

Building spatial awareness with attention inside and around the body in an action (using the six cardinal directions: above, below, side to side, front, and back) and across the midline of the body

Improving social relationships through team activities

PREPARE

- **Review Appendix A** *Notes and Background* to understand the purpose and how to deliver the lesson.

- **Hydrate** (See *Getting Started* page 33) and do the *Personal Bubbles and Home Breath* Lessons

- **Equipment:** Colored beanbags; spot markers (for younger children); nine cards, three each marked "OVER," "UNDER," and "AROUND," in different colors for each team.

- **Explain the rules:** Divide groups into teams of at least three participants per team and assign each team a color (beanbag).
  - Teams line up, and the first person in each team gets a beanbag.
  - A teacher, or one team member, stands in front of each team and holds up one card at a time. As he or she does, the team will yell out what is written on the card and follow the order. The teacher can demonstrate the movements ordered on the card to indicate how the beanbag should be passed down the team line (e.g. "OVER" card is held up and the bean bag should be passed *over* the head. When the UNDER card is held up, the beanbag should be passed *between* the knees; and when the AROUND card is held up, the beanbag should be passed_ around the side of the body. *See diagram above*).
  - The team member with the beanbag must pass the bag to the teammate behind him/her as directed by the card.
  - When the beanbag reaches the last person in the team line, he/she should run to the front of the line and begin the "order" from the next card.

GO!

Begin Over, Under, Around

o **Round One:** Every participant in the line has had a chance to pass the beanbag, according to the instruction on the cards. "OVER" is the first card.   When the whole team has passed the bean bag "OVER," and the first participant in the line again reaches the end of the line, the passing game repeats; but the instructions are based on the SECOND card (UNDER). Repeat the game using the third card (AROUND). When the final participant has received the beanbag, he/she should run to the head of the line, and the whole team must sit down and yell: "Done!"

o **Round Two:** The game can repeat as above, but instead of using a single instruction card for the whole team, the cards are alternated ("OVER," "UNDER," and "AROUND") until the whole team has responded to all three cards. This rotation can be done slowly at first and then can be speeded up to improve listening skills (even when excited).

CLOSING

Reflection is key to this lesson:

o Be sure to repeat hydration at end of this lesson.
o For young participants, ask: What do "over," "under," and "around" mean? Is the direction on the card referring to the relationship within your bodies - or the room?
o Help them understand that the meaning is always in relationship to the feeling of where their bodies are and where body parts are in relationship to other body parts.
o Ask older participants if it was easier or harder to follow the action with the change in instructions. What happens inside when the mind and actions change quickly?

NOTES & BACKGROUND

Why We Do Each Step in the Lesson:
To re-educate patterns of sensations

Background Behind Each Lesson:
Relevant research in sensations and perception

Part I – LESSON 1
PANCAKE BODY

NOTES
When We Do The Lesson
Condition: At the beginning and end of the day, before and after a lesson in order to sense and check-in on the effects of body-to-brain communication, before and after physical activity or recess

Behavior: Exercised but ungrounded, excited, imaginative, impatient, fidgety, unable to pay attention or listen

Why We Do the Lesson
o   Though *Pancake Body* will relax you, it is not a "relaxation" exercise. It is simple to do *but* difficult to comprehend the vast benefits until this lesson is practiced regularly.

o   The key to the lesson is directing *attention* to the *qualities of sensation in the body* using the floor as a "biofeedback" mechanism to get a clearer sense of pressure, weight, and integration of body parts against and off the floor.
   o   Subtle differences in sensation are felt more easily against a firm, smooth surface; the floor, for instance, becomes a neutral plane on which to sense where body parts are in relation to the whole. When body parts feel connected, they work better together.
   o   By sensing the body's position and shape, the nervous system starts re-educating itself and the mind becomes aware of how behavior locks into muscles.

o   Comparing the sensation of the body before and after movement lessons helps the brain understand what is going on in the body, even if we don't notice when the change happens.

   The ability to compare sensations before and after lessons expands understanding of how the body influences the mind. Feeling the differences in sensations increases awareness of this connection.

o   Awareness from *Pancake Body* helps synergize action and intention. Awareness of the subtlest (physical) changes in the body is the first step to increasing awareness of how our actions are often "doing" something different than what we intended.

o If participants are too hyperactive and are unable able to lie silently, have them notice the difficulty. Use the unsettled behavior as an assessment tool to compare the beginning to the ending of the lesson. Simply tell participants to notice if they are able to lie still and to check-in after the lesson.

However, sometimes bound-up energy in young bodies needs to be released before they are able to lie still. A pressure cooker needing to release steam is an analogy. Ask young children to run in place as fast as possible to release energy; young boys especially often need more aerobic activity before doing *Pancake Body*.

BACKGROUND

o *Pancake Body* deepens awareness of proprioceptive sense (what Sherrington called "the sixth sense"). This proprioceptive sense is foundational to forming perception.

o The lack of (neurological) awareness can make changes or improvements in the body or mind-set difficult to notice.

o When participants have a clear sense of subtle sensations, noticing how the body affects mental or emotional feelings is easier.

o Changing the position of the body's gravitational field from sitting to lying against the floor shifts alignment and makes it easier to notice behavioral patterns locked into muscular tension.

Part I – LESSON 2
PERSONAL BUBBLES FREEZE DANCE

NOTES
When We Do The Lesson
Condition: Issues with safety and respect, need for team building, lack of awareness in the body, or relationship to others, intruding, being oblivious to others physically or mentally

Behavior: Challenging social behavior, rudeness, disruptiveness, and being self-absorbed

Why We Do the Lesson
o This is a different kind of "personal bubble" exercise. The intention of this lesson is to change the focus of the senses from attending only to "out there" to gradually narrowing the senses to "who" keeps adjusting to "out there." Perception is a *sense* of time (what moves us) and space (orientation to life). Spatial awareness inside the body is a sensation of "who" is adjusting to demands and a sense of centeredness within those demands.

o Once participants are able to sense their *Personal Bubbles,* it is easier to sense within those bubbles. (Also see *Home Breath* lesson)
  o The senses of timing (or how we move) and spatial awareness (within the body) are both

fundamental to how the mind, mood, and body operate together.
- o Getting a sense within the body's spatial orientation also gives participants a concrete orientation to their relation to others and is foundational for team building.

- o *Personal Bubbles Freeze Dance* heightens attentiveness (to ourselves and others) and also to disciplinary measures.

    Associate the concept of feeling a "personal bubble" with listening; for example, relate the amount of space in a personal bubble to the space in which sound travels. This is very helpful especially for young children.

- o This lesson helps participants to understand, through experience, protocol for respect and responsibility in a classroom or work place, and in a fun and positive manner. (Also see *Listening Bubbles* and *Ho'oponopono Home*)

BACKGROUND
- o A "personal bubble" is literally a magnetic bubble that comes from the heart. Research at the Institute of HeartMath shows how the heart generates a strong, rhythmic, electromagnetic field around the body. This "bubble" can measure up to ten feet in diameter. The size of a personal bubble changes according to how close we feel toward another.

- o Behavior develops according to the spatial sense we have inside our personal bubbles. If we are "shy," we have a large bubble with little sense of "who" is inside; if we are "confident," we have a clearer sense of "who" is inside the bubble.

- o Running or jumping in place in the *Freeze Dance* refreshes the brain, calms the nervous system, and as a result improves memory. Professor John Ratey from Harvard University says; "Movement is crucial to all other brain functions – perception, attention, emotion – and affects the highest cognitive processes of memory, thinking, and learning" (Ratey, 2001, p. 175).

- o Without physical sensations we would have no memory. Dr. Candace Pert (and Dr. Moshe Feldenkrais) researched how memory is held throughout the body, not just in the brain (Madigan, 2000).

Part I – LESSON 3
PERSONAL BUBBLES & NO PLACE LIKE HOME BREATH

NOTES
When We Do The Lesson
> *Condition*: Before test taking or reading aloud, before challenging discussions, after recess, before doing presentations or public speaking engagements, overloaded, at the dentist's office

> *Behavior*: Anxiety, bumping into others, intruding, being oblivious to others

Why We Do The Lesson

o Key to *Home Breath* is that this is not a relaxation exercise. The intention of this breathing lesson is to feel the bodily sensation associated with difference in attitude after doing *Home Breath*. The sensation of *"Home"* is then used to recall the sense of centeredness under stress or in the height of emotional turbulence. In Hawaii "Home Breath" would be called "Pono Breath," pono means righteousness.

   o Both the long exhalations and the sound of "hommmmmme" or "haaaaaaaaaaaaaaaaaaa" will often bring a nervous system into a calmed, centered state of being.

   o Ask participants to notice the change in attitude after the breathing technique and how perception also changes with the body sensations. Awareness of subtle sensations of the body and how they affect the mind is key to understanding how our bodies affect thinking. Associating the feeling nature of the body (or emotions) to thinking helps learning.

o Also important to recognize: People may need to move or exercise to release energy before trying to get centered.

o Recommended: Introduce *Home Breath* through games and activities before using for disciplinary measures. Learning *"Home"* while having fun or being playful will inspire people to want to recall *"Home"* during challenging times.

o Look at the steps in the lesson. Attention, step-by-step, is narrowed from "out there" to inside oneself. Maintaining attention span is a challenge for many people; so in this lesson, we take their unfocused attention and attach it to the sensation of the breath and sound of *"Home"* to narrow attention inside and refresh the mind.

o Teaching *"Home"* to control children will only get short-term results. The sense of *"Home"* is a way of reasoning, learning, and understanding oneself; it is a way of life.

o A centered mind improves comprehension, memory, communication, listening, and awareness of the perception causing stress.

o Getting a sense of the body's "personal bubble" gives participants a sense of *where* to find *"Home"* inside. There are many lessons that teach breathing techniques but not a *sense* of orientation within the body associated with centeredness. The sensation of the body within its personal bubble is a guide to finding *"Home."*

o Conflict: If there is conflict between people, they will often have no sense of awareness inside the body. Remind them to shift attention to the memory of that *sensation* of *"Home"* and let that *"Home"* communicate to the other (See *Ho'oponopono Home*). If they don't remember how to shift their attention inside, please ask other participants for suggestions about how to remember and help each other.

o The concept of respect is easier to understand, especially for younger people, when they can *feel* the physical space between "personal bubbles."

o To associate this concept of "personal bubbles" with listening skills, see *Listening Bubbles* lesson.

o   Teachers and parents: Please do the lesson *with* your young people. Understanding the lesson is only possible through experience.

BACKGROUND

o   Disciplinary Measures: With the sense of space *inside* the body, mental acuity improves. But acquiring spatial awareness within oneself requires training. The clearer awareness is inside, the more one can be aware of someone else. Think about this when taking disciplinary measures with a child. If what is said is not comprehended, the child may have no sense of self and thus no sense of what is being explained. Perception comes from the physical sense of the body within the personal bubble.

o   Visceral sensations help us focus attention on "who" is being attentive instead of what is being attended to. Sensations are often captured by external influences and draw us out of our bodies and away from clear thinking. Attention to the visceral sensations of *"Home"* helps inhibit the overload of external stimuli. This inhibition of externals expands awareness of the individual, relieving reactions purely directed to others.

o   The combination of these two lessons is key to enhancing the proprioceptive sense (body orientation and synergy of the senses giving perception), which is the foundation of all learning.

o   Breath: The *No Place Like Home* section teaches that long exhalations slow the heart rate, calm emotions, and enhance mental acuity.
   o   Notice the rhythm of the breath, and learn what is happening within the body and mind. The rhythm of breathing changes with different types of actions, feelings, thoughts, and movements.
   o   One way to notice how children or adults are thinking and feeling is to watch the rhythm of their breathing. A tight ribcage or shallow, halted breathing can heighten emotional sensitivity. If we are confused when receiving directions, our breath may become shallow, or even halt temporarily. If we are feeling hesitant, we may want to notice if we are holding our breath.
   o   Exhaling deeply sends messages to the vagus nerve and can help calm the heart rate. "The information from the aortic body (the aorta is the largest blood vessel in the heart and connects to the orifice of the left ventricle of the heart) travels along the vagus nerve (the tenth cranial nerve) to the respiratory center. The vagus nerve contains thousands of nerve fibers, many of which also carry information between the heart to the brain" (Childre & Martin, 1999, p. 31).
   o   Breathing is one of the only functions that most people can perform voluntarily or involuntarily; therefore it crosses the bridge between the experience of the autonomic nervous system and the voluntary nervous system (or being able to consciously control breathing).

o   Breathing is intimately connected to the heart rate, emotions, and mental acuity. When breathing is used to find the sense of centeredness, perceptions shift. (Whenever the word "sense" is used, think of the physical sensation of the body.) According to Celia Lavatelli's book on *Piaget's Theory of Development* (Lavatelli, 1973): "Only when a child must, in some way, change what he perceives around him is logical thinking involved."

o   A *Personal Bubble* is really an energetic or magnetic field that surrounds the body. This field is able to be measured by scientists with biofeedback machines; it emanates from the heart. Experiencing the sensation of the boundary in this field can help an individual find his/her center. The interplay between feeling the differences from the "outer world" and from one's center is what the nervous system naturally does to learn.

> Brain and heart researchers at the Institute of HeartMath reported: "The heart's electromagnetic field is by far the most powerful produced by the body; it's approximately 5000 times greater in strength than the fields produced by the brain. It can be measured up to 8-10 feet away with sensitive detectors called magnetometers" (Childre and Martin, 1999, p. 33).

Part I – LESSON 4
NO PLACE LIKE HOME BREATH
(Also see Notes under Personal Bubbles & No Place Like Home Breath)

NOTES
When We Do The Lesson
Condition: Before test taking or reading aloud, after recess, before doing presentations or public speaking engagements, at the dentist's office

Behavior: Too energetic, fidgety, hyper, aggressive, nervous, anxious, feeling pressured, easily frustrated upon making mistakes, bored, poor posture, tired

Why We Do the Lesson
o Applying this lesson to life is key. The *Home* lesson is not just about getting calm. Remembering the sensation and state of mind with *Home* changes lives. Notice the perception in what we are doing or thinking when we lose the feeling of *Home*. Then ask: "Is this is a pattern or is it really how we feel away from insights of *Home*?"

> For example, when complaining, blaming, or arguing, take time to notice when the feeling of *Home* inside got lost. All attention, when blaming someone or something, is targeting "out there." Self-concept or responsibility is also missing. Feeling sensations in the core of the body *to* sense self is the first step to self-responsibility.

o The rhythm of breathing mirrors the physiological experiences of all types of actions, feelings, thoughts, and movements. Notice the rhythm and depth of your breathing; it may reveal something you didn't realize. If participants are confused while receiving directions, their breath may become shallow or temporarily halt. If there is a hesitation in the breath, take three or four long exhalations and see what may be revealed (that was not in awareness).

o With respect to focusing attention inside, first teach spatial awareness in relation to other people, then to the people and the room, and then to the participants' own bodies. This gives them a sense of *where* to find *"Home."* There are many lessons that teach breathing techniques to calm us, but if participants do not get a sense of orientation to their bodies and personal bubbles, it is challenging to find the center of their bodies with attention. (See *Personal Bubbles* lessons)

o *"Home Breath"* is also known in Hawaii as *"Pono Breath."* Pono means righteousness. Both the long exhalations and the sound of "hommmmmme" or "haaaaaaaaaaaaaaaaaaa" will bring a nervous system into a calmed, centered state. And most important: If participants need to move, allow them to exercise to release energy before trying to "calm" them. We highly recommend teaching the *Home Breath after* games or activities that are fun and playful.

o   Long exhalations with our *attention* to sensation deepen awareness of the connections among physical, mental, and emotional feelings. The change in these feelings before and after the *Home* lesson shows participants how the body influences the mind.

o   Two objectives in this lesson are: To give participants a technique *to find the feeling of centeredness* and to show how to *recall this feeling when eyes are open.* Sometimes asking participants how they remember this sensation of *Home* helps them recall *the mindset of Home* during their next upsetting or stressful time. (For example, one child automatically thought of the sensation of "chocolate mountains" in his heart to center himself so he could express what was wrong.)

o   Remembering how "*Home*" influences them will help participants use the technique during high-anxiety situations or before exams. If people get into conflicts, ask them if they can still feel their "*Home.*" If remembering the feeling of *Home* is difficult, ask participants: "How would communicating from this place help?"

o   *Attention* to sensations after long exhalations centers the mind and thus may also improve comprehension and memory.

o   If participants are hyper and need to rock on their bellies, transferring the *sensation of weight rocking* from one side of the body to the other against the floor can help center and calm anxious energy. This technique is similar to the primal instinct to calm a baby by rocking.

> Lying on the belly while doing the *Home Breath:* Rocking on the belly massages organs and can soothe back muscles, especially after sitting for long periods; it is best when done on a soft surface. The rocking motion is one of the most primal sensations that calm the nervous system. The sensation of weight shift (or proprioceptive sense of pressure shifting) from side to side through the midline helps trigger the body to center itself.

o   A tight ribcage or shallow halted breathing can heighten emotional sensitivity making small issues seem large.

BACKGROUND

o   Perception changes how we breathe, and breathing rhythms can change perception.

o   American teachers are set on raising the IQ of children, but a more realistic goal (according to Jean Piaget) is to develop intellectual competence and recognize that such factors as motivation and self-concept are involved in intellectual competence. (Lavatelli, 1973, p. 42). "*Home*" brings awareness of self.

o   Breath work improves awareness in the multiple levels of mind/body integration. A calm heart and centered mind enhance cognitive learning, comprehension, problem solving, and self-direction.

o   Breathing techniques are used in psychotherapy to help change behavior and can even relieve drug withdrawal symptoms.

o   The vagus nerve exchanges information from our hearts to our brains (and brains to hearts). Long exhalations slow the heart rate, which also centers and calms the nervous system and relieves stress. Exhaling deeply sends messages through the vagus nerve and calms the heart rate. The information from the "aortic body" travels along the vagus nerve to the respiratory center. "The vagus nerve contains thousands of nerve fibers, many of which also carry information from the heart to the brain" (Childre & Martin, 1999, p. 31). (Aortic is in reference to the orifice of the left ventricle of the heart. The vagus nerve is the tenth cranial nerve, an afferent (sensory) nerve communicating the state of the viscera influencing breathing behavior.)

o   Breathing is one of the only functions most people can do either voluntarily or involuntarily; therefore, it crosses the bridge between the experience of the autonomic nervous system and the voluntary nervous system (conscious and unconscious control of a function).

o   Notice the change in the body from the beginning to the end of the lesson. This helps enhance deeper awareness of a "body intelligence" called the proprioceptive sense (Sherrington's "sixth sense"). Subtle sensations in this proprioceptive sense help us feel the oneness between body and mind. Clarity of the physical intelligence in sensations (and where they originate in the body) deepens awareness, relieves stress, and improves learning.

Part I – LESSON 5
BIG TINY BUBBLES

NOTES
When We Do the Lesson
Condition: Beginning of school year, meeting new people, before group dynamics, before math lessons, before addition and subtraction lessons, when people are disrespectful

Behavior: Difficulty understanding one's personal effect on others, difficulty recognizing how intention is different from actions, difficulty respecting personal space, conflict resolution. (Also see *Ho'oponopono Home*)

Why We Do the Lesson
o   Our *sense* of self and how we perceive the world are intimately related to our attitudes (in our "big bubble" of awareness "out there"), and attitudes are inseparable from our alignment, or spatial organization, of body parts (inside our "tiny bubbles").

o   Though space around the body is difficult for a young child (and many adults) to sense, it is a stepping-stone in learning spatial awareness *inside the body.* For most people, the conscious awareness of what is utilized from within the body is only a small percentage of their potential. (Every year, human beings continue to improve in education, medicine, and physical performance.) We are constantly doing things we don't realize we are doing.   Being fully "human" means being in coherence or having the mind, body, and heart in resonance.

o   Leading movement with different body parts then maintaining a freezing position shows the mind which body part is directing the movement and is often surprising, even for adults.

o Respect has to do with spatial awareness within ourselves and with others. Knowing what we are actually doing compared to *what we think* we are doing begins with having an awareness of our internal dialogue (physical and mental) that is in relation to our environment.

o Increasing and decreasing the size of the imaginary bubble while moving to music enhances both exteroceptive perception (sight, hearing, touch, balance) and interoceptive perception (feedback solely from within the body).

o Awareness of perception (sense of self) and awareness of how we communicate are interrelated. Communication gaps happen when we are unaware of the fact that others misinterpret our words. Unintentional and disrespectful actions can be cleared up when our awareness recognizes the limits of how we perceive others.

o Communication challenges happen when we are sharing something totally different from what we are actually intending to share. People don't think sensory awareness of body parts has anything to do with communication; however, the reality is that the symbiotic organization of movement in the body forms how we perceive.

o The biological development of spatial awareness inside and around the body is foundational for cognitive development. Space and time are relevant to everything, even to learning reading and math, i.e., the letters of a word, patterns of a sentence, and numbers of a timetable. It may be easy to understand how spatial awareness is related to math, but spatial awareness can also affect how the mind interprets words according to where the words are on a page or in the structure of a sentence .

o Giving younger participants personal contexts in which to understand math can be done with the *Big Tiny Bubbles* lesson. Measurements such as volumes (inside a bubble), quantities (number of bubbles) and relationships of parts to a whole are associated with spatial organization.
  o Turn the bubbles into cubes and calculate that volume.
  o How would space change when you increase or decrease bubble sizes?

BACKGROUND
o *How* the mind biologically learns involves integrating information between the inside and the outer environment. For many people, this happens without awareness. Attention alternates between physical sensations and intentions, attitudes, and emotions. Ping-pong attention, within and then outside the body, on what we physically feel and what is going on in the body or mind, integrates our awareness of the connection among intention, sensation and action.

Part I – LESSON 6
LISTENING BUBBLES

NOTES:

When We Do the Lesson

> *Condition*: Establishing protocol for listening, transition times, need to get attention after recess or exciting activity
>
> *Behavior*: Trouble paying attention, poor posture, tired, energetic, bored, fidgety, hyperactive, aggressive, nervous, anxious, flustered when making mistakes

Why We Do the Lesson

o *Listening Bubbles* teaches respect and hearing from the "heart" space.

o Doing the *Personal Bubbles* lesson before *Listening Bubbles* helps participants understand sound on a physical level and how the sound they make travels and affects others.

> o *Personal Bubbles* gives participants the physical experience of how we affect each other by deepening spatial awareness. The physical *feeling* of this space between people is much easier for them to understand than the area of space sound covers while speaking.
>
> o Spatial awareness is foundational for all learning. Spatial awareness is inseparable from good listening skills, attention, how we interpret what is happening around us, and how we *orient* our perception.

o Recognizing different perspectives (shifting that occurs when the internal dialogue of our minds transitions to another's circumstances) is crucial to listening. We may notice words but not what they convey because too much of our own commentary is getting in the way. (See *Ho'oponopono Home* lesson)

o Understanding what people say and what they mean to say, or what people say and what others understand, requires listening bubbles of compassion and respect.

o When attention is directed into our hearts while listening, the mind calms and the ears open.

o Remind people about *Listening Bubbles* if there is a disruption in the classroom or workplace or if people are talking at the same time.

BACKGROUND

o The internal dialogue of anxiety or physical discomfort may also cause challenges associated with listening. Researchers Alfred Tomatis and Christian Vold focus more on the problems of "listening" than "hearing". A good deal of brain activity is the work of "silent" traffic - involuntary processes of function from the metabolism to a complex matrix of perceptions integrating taste, smell, touch, proprioception, and so on (Robinson, 2001, p. 99).

Part I – LESSON 7
BODY BUBBLES

NOTES
When We Do the Lesson

Condition: Need for improved safety through understanding the physical relationship to others, poor sense of space within the body, introduction to a new environment

Behavior: Challenged social behavior, disregard for others, shyness, low self-esteem, difficulty understanding and expressing feelings

Why We Do the Lesson

o To get a clearer *sense* of size and space within the body, we compare (with a string) the length of a participant's arm span to his/her height. The length of the string gives participants a new sense of height.

o Getting a sense of the internal space between body parts also clarifies awareness of how we think, act, and feel. Even many adults cannot feel 95 percent of their bodies or their actions aligned with intentions.

o Sensations connect thinking to action. Through sensations, the nervous system forms a network of patterns and movements. Patterns of *how* we do something (versus *what* we do) form self-esteem, perception, and social dynamics. Behavioral patterns of thinking, feeling, and acting are locked into our muscle patterns.

o Perception begins to develop through the symbiotic relationship of body, mind, and environment. *Sensory Self-Awareness* develops synergistically with all three. Thus, neurological patterning of physical *motion* develops in accordance with all three as well. And the experience of *Sensory Self-Awareness* is discovered by feeling the quality of movement.

o *Body Bubbles* enhances the awareness of how bones and muscles work together. As the body tires or feels stress, it contracts into familiar patterns wired into musculo-skeletal tension. These reactive patterns of muscle tension drain energy. It takes more work when patterns of muscular tension hold a posture than it does when we depend on our bones for strength and stability.

BACKGROUND

o The *Feldenkrais Method*® uses sensory-motor feedback, giving the brain the sense of where the bones are to re-educate the patterns of muscular tension and attitude.

o Lack of awareness on the inside can be measured by the capacity to sense the skeleton. As we age, we stop using our bones to support our posture: this is one of the reasons that osteoporosis is so prevalent in older women and men.

Part I – LESSON 8
HOKEY POKEY BODY BUBBLE

NOTES
When We Do the Lesson

Condition: To improve spatial awareness of body, to relate parts to a whole, to explore concepts of addition or subtraction, to demonstrate symmetry

Behavior: Scattered attention, boredom, chaotic energy, nervousness

Why We Do the Lesson

o   Repeating movements on the same side several times allows the brain/body to clearly sense and compare sensations from one side of the body to the other. The nervous system learns where to find "center" by feeling the differences from one side to the other side. Feeling differences among sensations of body parts is the most fundamental way that the body and mind learn.

o   *Sensory Self-Awareness* of body parts and the functional relationships among parts expands awareness of "self" - physically, mentally, and emotionally. This awareness facilitates an efficient way of moving and promotes a clearer sense of self-management.

o   Moving *attention* from one half to the equal and opposite half of the body (in *Hokey Pokey* steps) improves awareness *from* the body to the brain and enhances the ways in which parts of the body work together. When attention notices the sensations of how body parts work as a whole, our bodies find balance and grace. The experience of balance improves both physical coordination and emotional stability *if* attention is focused on the relationship between sensing and thinking.

o   The sense of motion in muscles, weight, and position in space is known as the "sixth sense" - or the proprioceptive sense. Without it, we wouldn't be able to sense we were in a body. The sense of self and the space inside the body is essential to the quality of developmental functioning, sensory-motor integration, and perception.

BACKGROUND

o   Crossing attention from one side of the body to the other through the midline improves centeredness of both mind and body. Dr. Paul Denison of BrainGym® and Dr. Carla Hannaford, neurophysiologist and author of *Smart Moves*, share the belief that movement crossing through the midline (by doing cross-lateral movement) also improves functioning and energizes the brain.

o   Self-awareness begins with one's relationship to the environment, and the most immediate environment is the body. The brain and nervous system develop synergistically with the organic nature of the body and its environment.

o   Sensing equal and opposites sides of the 6 cardinal directions (1. Right, 2. Left, 3. Front, 4. Back, 5. Above, 6. Below) is what the nervous system discerns in order to find balance and coordination. Over nineteen senses (Hannaford, 2002) send signals from the body to the brain: "Signals from this sensory motor orchestration are sent by afferent nerves through the spinal cord to the somatosensory, motor, and parietal cortices of the brain, where they continuously feed and update dynamic sensory-motor maps of the body" (Smetacek & Mechsner, 2004, p. 21).

o "Differentiate" refers to a physical sensation of measurement that assesses differences in how a neurological function changes as its input changes. To use differentiation to re-educate the nervous system, for example: If we injure ourselves and feel the sensations of the injury in our imagination on the healthy side of our bodies, the injured side will start to improve.

Part I – LESSON 9
DANCIN' HULA-HOOPS

NOTES
When We Do the Lesson

Condition: Fatigue, need for conflict resolution, tired from sitting for long periods of time

Behavior: Fidgety, excited, hyperactive, inattentive to directions, anxious, desiring movement

Why We Do the Lesson

o The lesson starts with a sitting twist in order to measure awareness of the differences in the body (and attitude) before and after the lesson.

o This lesson helps to reduce stiffness in the spinal column, increase mobility from core muscles, and expand spatial awareness.

o Starting with one hula hoop and then gradually adding more hoops will tip and angle the movement of the spine. Small intricate movements throughout the vertebral joints slightly change the rotation of the spine, which helps release hard-to-access areas of tension along the spinal column.

o Spiral rotational movement in the spine is beneficial to the ease and grace of all other movements and for postural alignment.

BACKGROUND

o This is an easy and fast lesson to refresh children's minds. Participants who sit for more than 20 minutes at a time can experience a decrease in the flow of the brain-derived neurotropic factor (BDNF), according to kinesiologist Jean Blaydes Madigan. BDNF helps enable one neuron to communicate with another (Madigan, 2000).

o Directing *attention* to the *movement sensations in the body* from the spinning hula hoops magnifies internal and external spatial awareness and heightens the orientation of proprioceptive awareness. The proprioceptive sense is what orients the relationship of body parts in space, creating a sense of perception.

o Signals from the sensory-motor and attention orchestrate (multiple hula-hoops moving) and send different sensations of impulses to the somatosensory, motor, and parietal cortices of the brain. There, they continuously feed and update the dynamic sensory-motor maps of the body.

o Option to make the relay longer: Nonstop aerobic exercise for a minimum of 12 minutes has been found to be beneficial for quicker cognitive responses, processing information, memory, and problem solving (Etnier, et. al., 1999; Van Boxtel, et. al., 1996; as cited in Madigan, 2000, p. 15).

Part I – LESSON 10
HULA RELAY

NOTES
When We Do the Lesson

Condition: Needing to re-charge, needing to learn respect for personal space of self and others, before a math lesson

Behavior: Fidgety, excited, hyper, not paying attention to directions

Why We Do the Lesson

o Sprints and aerobic exercise recharge the brain and body.

o Running around the hoops and dodging others increases agility, balance, spatial awareness, and teamwork. More important, it helps increase respect for fellow participants.

o Holding a hula hoop while running around hoops on the ground expands awareness of the space immediately around the body and the sense of relationship to others and the environment.

o Our sense of identity begins to form with the sense of spatial awareness; what is around us and *inside of us*. Taking steps to narrowing attention to smaller and smaller areas around the body helps to organically tune our attention and refocus it inside. In the lesson, attention and the senses are conditionally directed to the physical space around us to teach awareness of *where* attention is pointed.

o The movement of tipping from side to side while running around hoops on the ground initiates spiral rotation on lateral sides of the spinal column which influences movement for better posture, alignment, and spatial orientation.

o Balancing and agility activities can help with reading lessons. (See *Background* below.)

o Timing relays and associating times with learning addition, subtraction, multiplication, or division help children to understand how math can serve us even when we are having fun. When setting up the game, ask children to count off and then ask them to divide themselves into two or three teams. Applying math equations to life situations will help long-term learning and inspire participants to learn more about mathematics.

o Also see Notes and Background under *Big Tiny Bubbles* lesson.

BACKGROUND

o Hula hoops twirling around the body while running provide spatial awareness challenges. Awareness in and around the body heightens the sense of proprioception (which orients the "sense" among body parts within the body). The intention of the steps in the game is to gently narrow attention toward the spatial awareness from around the body into the core of the body.

o Twisting, bending, and rotating are all part of a spiral rotation that happens in the spinal column. The spiral rotation movement is a primary movement for all living things and is central to developmental movements. (Recommendation: Follow this lesson with *Fish Roll* in *Part II.*)

o Participants who sit for more than 20 minutes at a time can experience a decrease in the flow of the brain-derived neurotropic factor (BDNF), according to kinesiologist Jean Blaydes Madigan. BDNF also helps one neuron to communicate with another (Madigan, 2000).

o Sense of balance has been associated with levels of reading capacity, according to Madigan. In her book *Thinking on Your Feet*, she says: "These systems (vestibular and cerebellum systems for balance and motor activity) keep our balance, turn thinking into action, and coordinate moves." (Madigan, 2004, p. 15).

o Option to make the relay longer: Nonstop, aerobic exercise for a minimum of 12 minutes was found to be beneficial for quicker cognitive responses, processing information, memory, and problem solving (Etnier, et.al., 1999; *Van Boxtel, et.al.,* 1996; as cited in Madigan, 2000, p. 15).

Part I – LESSON 11
HO'OPONOPONO HOME

NOTES
When We Do the Lesson
Condition: Establishing protocol, conflict resolution, difficulty communicating

Behavior: Angry, upset, sad, withdrawn because of interaction with another.

Why We Do the Lesson

o *Ho'oponopono Home* deepens the consciousness of self-responsibility during communication breakdowns.

o From the sensation of *"Home"* inside, the mind's perspective opens - and so does the heart. For this process of communication to be of significant value, it needs to be adapted into life at home, work, or classroom.

o It is recommended to do *Pono Breath* or *Home Breath* (*"Pono"* and *"Home"* are interchangeable) before this lesson. This lesson is more than just making the sound of "Hommmmme" or the sound of "Haaaaaaaaaaaaaaaaa;" it is also imagining the feeling of letting go while making these sounds. Directing attention to the sensation traveling deep inside gives the mind a sense of centeredness, thus participants listen from the heart while communicating.

o The technique of the lesson reveals hidden agendas during communication. When participants feel inside the body while listening, they recognize their internal commentary - and their interpretation of external commentary comes from the heart. From educator and therapist Harville Hendrix's website: "We can begin to co-operate with this hidden agenda. As a result, we can choose to grow together in a creative, non-controlling, and healing way that creates understanding and connection." - Harville Hendrix

o *Ho'oponopono* has been used for centuries in the Hawaiian culture to improve human relationships and kindness of heart. Ho'oponopono means "mental cleansing" and was used in family conferences where relationships were set right through prayer, discussion, confession, repentance, and mutual restitution and forgiveness (Pukui, Elbert, 1986).

o Ponopono is defined as: "To put to rights, to put in order or shape, correct, amend, regulate, and arrange." Pono is defined as: "Goodness, uprightness, morality, moral qualities, correct or proper procedure, excellence, well-being, prosperity, welfare, benefit, true condition or nature, duty, moral, fitting, proper, righteous, right, upright, just, virtuous, fair, beneficial, successful, in perfect order, accurate, correct, eased, relieved, should, ought, must, necessary" (Pukui, Elbert, 1986).

o From the *Center for Non-Violent Communication (NVC)* website: "All that has been integrated into NVC has been known for centuries about consciousness, language, communication skills, and use of power that enable us to maintain a perspective of empathy for ourselves and others, even under trying conditions." -- Marshall B. Rosenberg, PhD.

o This lesson is based on the teachings of *Ho'oponopono*, *Home Breath* lesson, Harville Hendrix's work and the *NVC* techniques. (See *Background* following this lesson.)

o For those who have completed *Part I*
  o See if participants apply anything they have learned in problem solving, self-direction, or leadership skills. Maybe some are doing the *Home Breath* and other calming movements related to development. Note the children who isolate themselves or become more extroverted. Is this a common occurrence for those children?
  o For the heart to reach the mind, doing Part I lessons in this order is highly recommended.

  Part I

1. *Pancake Body*	2. *Home Breath and Personal Bubbles*	3. *Personal Bubbles Freeze Dance*
4. *Big Tiny Bubbles*	5. *Listening Bubbles*	6. *Body Bubbles*

BACKGROUND
o As mentioned above, this lesson is also based on two techniques of communication: Ho'oponopono and *Non-violent Communication* (NVC). In the process of NVC, participants identify differences in how they feel and learn to acknowledge the other in a compassionate manner. The ability to be compassionate, really listen, and communicate from another's perspective takes a heightened sense of self-awareness.

o Children and adults alike can listen better when they feel they have been heard. When there is "no blame" and "no fault" but an acknowledgment of differences, emotional charge and violence are diffused. The barriers of emotional upset are lightened, if not totally lifted.

o   When the *whole* muscular pattern that is distorted is released, even on a purely physical level, perception shifts, and it is easier to feel compassion and non-judgment.

o   Cross-reference the dynamics that happen between people and the dynamics that happen within our selves. The effect *Ho'oponopono Home* has between two people is similar to how habitual patterns of behavior affect musculo-skeletal patterns. One person's attitude influences the other person's way of communicating. Habitual patterns in muscles influence the behavior of the brain; we think what we feel is true and not necessarily what is going on with someone else or in the current situation.

o   The NVC method has been used by Fred Burks, a personal language interpreter, to improve communication at the White House in Washington, D.C., in meetings with Presidents Clinton and G. W. Bush, Vice Presidents Cheney and Gore, and other dignitaries.

Part I – LESSON 12
OVER, UNDER, AROUND

NOTES:
When We Do the Lesson
   Condition: Transition times, after long periods sitting, when people need to exercise, before geometry, for physical education class

   Behavior: Lack of attention or focus, burnt out, overloaded, tired

Why We Do the Lesson
o   Younger children have a difficult time knowing where their bodies are in space. This is one of the reasons they have a hard time behaving while in a line or when asked to respect each other (be "pono" as Hawaiians say). By passing a beanbag with attention to the action of "over, under and around," participants get a sense of orientation to their bodies versus orientation to the room.

o   This is an important lesson for younger children - or people who don't sense the difference between outside, around, and inside their bodies. Our tendencies are to orient ourselves strictly from the environment and not *ourselves to* the environment. Being self-reliant or responsible would be difficult if perception was oriented solely "out there."
   o   This lesson accentuates the importance of noting how the mind orients itself to the body or to others. Western perception is normally initiated from "out there" versus inside ourselves.
   o   For example, if a directive was given to put your hand above your head while lying on the ground where would your hand go? Try it. Did your hand go towards the ceiling or towards the wall the crown of your head is facing? If your hand goes toward the ceiling, your mind orients you to the environment more than from within. If your hand goes toward the wall the crown of your head is facing, your mind orients you from within your body.

BACKGROUND

o Perception is relative to our sense of physical space in and around the body. Participants' interpretation of movement directions can show how individual perception is subconsciously oriented to "out there."

> Educational Science is designed to train students' attention to focus outside themselves for long periods of time. There is very little training on turning attention and focus inside. The amount of time we are trained to do something will determine if perception becomes conditioned to do it automatically. If we only train our attention to focus "out there" (at the teacher) for answers, when "out there" doesn't work, neither will we.

SUPPORTING SCHOOL NEEDS

SPECIFIC SCHOOL NEEDS THAT LESSONS SUPPORT

School Needs
Attention
    Attention
    Focus
    Listening
Developmental
Higher Order
    Cross Lateral Movements
    Self-Awareness
    Self-Awareness with Others
    Spatial Awareness of Body
    Spatial Awareness of Others
Math
    Addition and Subtraction
    Geometry
    Spatial Awareness
    Symmetry
Memory
Neuromuscular Re-education
    Neuromuscular Re-education
    Alignment
Social
    Communication Skills

    Conflict Resolution
    Discipline
    Respect
    Safety
    Social Behavior
    Teamwork
Stress Reduction
    Calming
    Centering
    Recharge
    Relaxation
    Self-Awareness
    Stress Reduction
Transition Times
    Passive
    Active

Legend
    Active: Very physical, aerobic
    Body: Neuromuscular re-education
    Passive: Non-aerobic in classroom
    Transitions Times (TT): In classroom
    Need Room: Requires floor space

	Active	Passive	TT	Body	Need Room	Page No.
ATTENTION						
Attention						
Hokey Pokey Body Bubble				X		54
Home Breath & Personal Bubbles		X	X			44
Pancake Body		X	X	X		40

	Active	Passive	TT	Body	Need Room	Page No.
Focus						
Hokey Pokey Body Bubble		X	X			54
Home Breath		X	X			46
Listening						
Hokey Pokey Body Bubble		X	X			54
Listening Bubbles		X	X			50
Over, Under, Around		X	X			62
Pancake Body		X	X	X		40
DEVELOPMENTAL						
(Also see Part II of Wellness Through Movement®)						
Big Tiny Bubbles	X					48
Body Bubbles		X	X			52
Dancin' Hula Hoops	X					56
Ho'oponopono Home		X	X			60
Hokey Pokey Body Bubble		X	X			54
Home Breath & Personal Bubbles		X	X			44
Listening Bubbles		X	X			50
No Place Like Home Breath		X	X			46
Over, Under, Around		X	X			62
Pancake Body		X				40
Personal Bubbles & No Place Like Home Breath		X	X			44
HIGHER-ORDER FUNCTION						
Cross Lateral Movements						
Big Tiny Bubbles	X					48
Hula Relay Personal Bubbles	X					58
Self-Awareness						
(Higher-order Function)						
Body Bubbles		X	X			52
Big Tiny Bubbles				X	X	48
Hokey Pokey Body Bubble			X	X		54

	Active	Passive	TT	Body	Need Room	Page No.
Ho'oponopono P.E.		X	X			60
No Place Like Home Breath		X	X			46
Pancake Body		X	X	X		40
Personal Bubbles & No Place Like Home Breath		X	X			44
Self-Awareness with Others						
(Higher-order Function)						
Big Tiny Bubbles				X	X	48
Body Bubbles		X	X	X		52
Hokey Pokey Body Bubble		X	X	X		54
Hula Relay Personal Bubbles				X	X	58
Personal Bubbles Freeze Dance		X	X	X		42
Spatial Awareness of Body						
Body Bubbles		X	X	X		52
Hokey Pokey Body Bubble	X		X	X		54
Personal Bubbles Freeze Dance	X		X	X		42
Spatial Awareness of Others						
(Also see Self-Awareness with Others)						
Big Tiny Bubbles				X	X	48
Body Bubbles		X	X	X		52
Dancin Hula Hoops	X			X	X	56
Hula Relay Personal Bubbles	X			X	X	58
Over, Under, Around		X	X	X		62
MATH						
Addition and Subtraction						
Hula Relay Personal Bubbles				X	X	58
Geometry						
Big Tiny Bubbles	X		X	X		48
Spatial Awareness						
Big Tiny Bubbles	X		X	X		48

	Active	Passive	TT	Body	Need Room	Page No.
Hokey Pokey Body Bubble		X	X	X		54
Symmetry						
Hokey Pokey		X	X	X		54
Over, Under, Around		X	X	X		62
Pancake Body		X	X	X		40
MEMORY						
Personal Bubbles Freeze Dance	X		X	X		42
No Place Like Home Breath		X	X			46
NEUROMUSCULAR RE-EDUCATION						
Neuromuscular Re-education						
Pancake Body		X	X	X	X	40
Alignment						
(Also see Posture & Attention)						
Pancake Body		X	X	X	X	40
SOCIAL						
Communication Skills						
Ho'oponopono P.E.		X	X			60
Personal Bubbles & No Place Like Home Breath		X	X			44
Conflict Resolution						
Personal Bubbles & No Place Like Home Breath		X	X			44
Ho'oponopono P.E.		X	X			60
Discipline						
Ho'oponopono Home		X	X			60
Listening Bubbles		X	X			50
No Place Like Home Breath		X	X			46

	Active	Passive	TT	Body	Need Room	Page No.
Personal Bubbles & No Place Like Home Breath		X	X			44
Personal Bubbles Freeze Dance	X		X	X		42
Respect						
Body Bubbles		X	X	X		52
Ho'oponopono P.E.		X	X			60
Listening Bubbles		X	X			50
Personal Bubbles & No Place Like Home Breath		X	X			44
Personal Bubbles Freeze Dance	X		X	X	X	42
Safety						
(See P.E. Lessons)						
Body Bubbles		X	X	X		52
Dancin' Hula Hoops	X					56
Hula Relay Personal Bubble	X					58
Personal Bubbles & No Place Like Home		X	X			44
Personal Bubbles Freeze Dance	X		X	X		42
Social Behavior						
Ho'oponopono P.E.		X	X			60
Over, Under, Around		X	X	X	X	62
Teamwork						
Over, Under, Around		X	X	X	X	62
Personal Bubbles Freeze Dance	X					42
STRESS REDUCTION						
Calming						
(See Relaxation)						
Personal Bubbles & No Place Like Home Breath		X	X			44
No Place Like Home Breath		X	X			46
Centering						
Dancin' Hula Hoops	X		X			56

	Active	Passive	TT	Body	Need Room	Page No.
Hula Relay Personal Bubbles	X			X		58
No Place Like Home Breath		X	X			46
Pancake Body		X	X	X		40
Personal Bubbles & No Place Like Home Breath		X	X			44
Recharge						
Dancin' Hula Hoops	X					56
Hula Relay Personal Bubbles	X			X		58
Pancake Body	X		X	X		40
Relaxation						
No Place Like Home Breath		X	X			46
Pancake Body		X	X	X		40
Self-Awareness						
(Also see Stress Reduction)						
Body Bubbles		X	X	X		52
Big Tiny Bubbles	X		X	X		48
Personal Bubbles & No Place Like Home Breath		X	X			44
Pancake Body		X	X	X		40
Stress Reduction						
Personal Bubbles & No Place Like Home		X	X			44
No Place Like Home Breath		X	X			46
TRANSITION TIMES						
Passive						
Ho'oponopono Home		X	X			60
No Place Like Home Breath		X	X			46
Listening Bubbles		X	X			50
Personal Bubbles & No Place Like Home		X	X			44
Active						
Over, Under, Around		X	X	X		62

GLOSSARY

ADD refers to Attention Deficit Disorder. Those with ADD have difficulty paying attention to details, following instructions, and organizing tasks, and they are often categorized as being easily distracted.

ADHD refers to Attention Deficit Hyperactivity Disorder; difficulties in focusing accompanied by hyperactive behavior.

Aerobic refers to movement when the body requires more air due to the activity being performed.

Afferent nerves carry nerve impulses from receptors or sense organs toward the central nervous system – compared to efferent nerves that carry impulses away from the central nervous system, otherwise known as motor neurons.

Awareness is categorized by anthropologists on four levels:
1. Awareness of physical form
2. Awareness splitting mind and body (sensory and self awareness)
3. ***Awareness of mind and body as inseparable***
4. Awareness of mind, body, and spirit inseparable

This book refers primarily to level three, awareness of mind and body as inseparable; a mindfulness and wisdom in the ability to sense and to be conscious of sensory-motor patterns symbiotically creating perception, or an individual's biological perception of his/her mind.

Bodily Kinesthetic refers to when learners learn best by moving their bodies.

Cognition is the process of thought and how one processes information; trying to make sense of the world.

Core muscles refers to muscle-initiated actions from the center of the body specifically related to the spinal column (core muscles also provide stronger force and stability).

Dynamic means relating to forces, energy, or objects producing motion.

Feldenkrais Method® is an educational system centered on movement that aims to improve the quality of "Self" through awareness.

Heart refers to the sense of centeredness and compassion in the *mind*.

Home refers to a sense of centeredness from the heart and fuels the sense of self-responsibility and awareness of one's own personal process; a place of safety inside and understanding of oneself.

Ho'oponopono refers to making it right, coming from righteousness, taking 100 percent responsibility for your own actions, management, and development in self-awareness.

Hyperactivity refers to fidgety behavior, excessive desire to talk or move around, and the tendency to blurt out answers.

Internal dialogue is the dialogue that weaves the profound functions of the (biological) self and the relationship to external compositions into an interconnected whole.

IQ, or intelligence quotient, is a score derived from one of many different standardized tests; originally measured by Francis Galton (founder of modern psychological measurement) through sensory acuity of the level of pressure, light, heat, et cetera, that an individual can sense (Gardner, 1999).

Kinesthesia is the muscular sense perception through motion.

Nervous System is a network of specialized cells that correlates or communicates information from both internal and external environments to operate the whole organism; includes the spinal cord, brain, and nerves throughout the body.

Neuro refers to concepts or topics related to the brain or nervous system.

Neuron refers to a nerve cell or excitable cell in the nervous system that transmits information from one cell to another through electrochemical impulses.

NVC stands for *Non-Violent Communication*, a technique of communication based on principles of nonviolence - the natural state of compassion when no violence is present in the heart. (See www.cnvc. org); method was created by Marshall Rosenberg

Parietal cortices of the brain refers to areas of the brain positioned posterior to the frontal lobe and above (superior to) the occipital lobe located at the base of the skull.

PART I A NEW SENSORY SELF-AWARENESS **Tools to Experience Body-to-Brain Communication:** This dynamic and interactive series of twelve lessons shows participants how to feel the influence their bodies have on thinking and feeling. The program is designed to improve awareness, in-classroom management, and school culture. Participants learn how to shift perception from outside to inside by developing a clearer sense of self and their relationship with others. An array of self-observing techniques using breath, sound, and movement promote awareness of mental, emotional and physical interconnections. *A New* Sensory *Self Awareness* helps lives change.

PART II YOUNG AT HEART P.E. **For the Heart, Body and Mind:** This in-depth series of twenty neuromuscular reeducation movement games is based on the *Feldenkrais Method*®, developmental movements and the National Physical Education Standards for elementary grades. The program uses alignment, attitude, and quality of movement to expand perception. Games also target the physical and emotional challenges that narrow attention or fuel problem behaviors. *Young At Heart P.E.* organizes the stimulus of motor patterns that contribute to self-perception.

PART III MOVEMENT FOR THE LEARNER **In-Classroom Curriculum:** This series of fifty-two in-classroom sensory-movement lessons is designed to enhance brain functioning and improve performance in language arts and mathematics. More important, the lessons aid in the development of social skills, attention skills, and higher order skills. These lessons are designed to also increase physical comfort for people while seated at a desk or when they are required to have long attention spans. *Movement for the Learner In-Classroom Curriculum* integrates the studies of the *Feldenkrais Method®*, cognitive development theories, and stages of sensory-motor development.

Perception refers to a conscious sensory experience (Goldstein, 2007); the process of attaining awareness or understanding through experience; and how sensory information translates the internal and external worlds of the perceiver.

Perceptual process refers to "a sequence of steps leading from the environment to perception of a stimulus, recognition of the stimulus and action with regard to the stimulus" (Goldstein, 2007).

Personal space refers to the spherical field created by the magnetic field of the heart.

Physical sensation refers to the sensations within the body beneath the skin, associated with emotions, physical parts of the body, and motion.

Pono in Hawaiian refers to righteousness or the sense of "home," centeredness, and goodness inside.

Proprioception is one's own perception based on biological and cognitive stages of development; insight; "sixth sense" (Charles Sherrington, neurophysiologist) or extrasensory perception; the sense of the relative position of neighboring parts of the body to the whole self; gut feeling, attitude of posture and quality of moving.

Magnetic field refers to the spherical magnetic field produced by the heart that can reach up to ten feet in diameter.

MOVEMENT FOR THE LEARNER **In-Classroom Curriculum** is Part III of the Wellness Through Movement program. This series of fifty-two in-classroom sensory-movement lessons is designed to enhance brain functioning and improve performance in language arts and mathematics. More important, the lessons aid in the development of social skills, attention skills, and higher order skills. These lessons are designed to also increase physical comfort for people while seated at a desk or when they are required to have long attention spans. *Movement for the Learner In-Classroom Curriculum* integrates the studies of the *Feldenkrais Method®*, cognitive development theories, and stages of sensory-motor development.

Self is the observer of one's own perception based on the deep internal sensation of the proprioceptive sense.

Sensation refers to the operation of the 19 senses, primarily the common five senses - sight, touch, taste, smell, hearing - and the proprioceptive sense or extrasensory perception based on the sensation of physical parts of the body and their orientations. (*Also see* proprioception.)

Sensory acuity refers to sharpness or keenness in sensing subtle levels of sensations, such as weight or pressure, brightness of light, volumes of sound, and degrees of muscle tension.

Sensory deprivation is a deliberate reduction or removal of one or more senses.

Sensory-motor map refers to the dynamics of programming from patterns of integration between the motor and sensory functioning in both the brain and body.

Sensory Self-Awareness is *a neutral mode of observation (in this context) from physical sensations* dependent on thoughts and emotions. (*See* Awareness.)

Somatosensory refers to having sensory activity elsewhere other than in the special sense organs (such as the eyes or ears) conveying information about the state of the body and its immediate environment.

Somatic refers to relating to or affecting the body (Webster, 1993); the symbiotic or interdependent relationship of voluntary and involuntary body movements associated with external stimuli that help to keep the body and mind in touch with surroundings (e.g., touch, hearing, balance, sight, etc.) and consists of efferent nerves responsible for sending signals of muscle contraction to the brain.

Spatial awareness refers to the deduction of distance, rate of speed, or comparative parts or sides with immediate environment *or* within the walls of the body.

Symbiotic refers to having an interdependent relationship with two or more parts.

Synergy occurs when two or more parts operate together and produce an effect greater than the sum of individual parts; "synergistic" refers to the effect of synergy.

Traditional Treatments for ADHD: Psychotherapy (set strategies to handle feelings), medication (to sedate or stimulate in order to regulate neurotransmitters in the brain), strong support systems, and punishment (time out or more severe).

Virtue refers to the standard of goodness or "right action," based on physical sensations of equanimity (or from the "heart").   Virtue and physical sensations are an interwoven maze (like perception and action). Cascades of neurological impulses from the body/mind functionally integrate to provide perception "a physical sense" of what is virtuous.

Young at Heart P.E. is the name of Part II of the *Wellness Through Movement*® program. This in-depth series of twenty neuromuscular reeducation movement games is based on the *Feldenkrais Method*®, developmental movements and the National Physical Education Standards for elementary grades. The program uses alignment, attitude, and quality of movement to expand perception. Games also target the physical and emotional challenges that narrow attention or fuel problem behaviors. *Young At Heart P.E.* organizes the stimulus of motor patterns that contribute to self-perception.

REFERENCES

BOOKS

Armstrong, T. (1998). *Awakening Genius in the Classroom.* Alexandria, VA: Association of Supervision and Curriculum Development.

Bailey, B. (2000). *Conscious Discipline.* Oviedo, FL: Loving Guidance, Inc.

Berne, S. A. (1994). *Creating Your Personal Vision.* Santa Fe, NM: Color Stone Press.

Bohm, D. (1988). *David Bohm Dialogues, Ojai 1988,* Ojai CA: David Bohm Seminars.

Boring, E. (1933). *The Physical Dimensions of Consciousness,* New York, NY: The Century Company.

Bower, T.G.R. (1941). *A Primer of Infant Development.* San Francisco, CA: W.H. Freeman and Company.

Braden, G. (2006). *Secrets of the Lost Mode of Prayer.* New York, NY: City: Hayhouse.

Chasnoff, I. (2001). *The Nature of Nurture.* Chicago, IL: Exponent Publishers, Inc.

Childre, D., & Martin, H. (1999). *The HeartMath Solution.* San Francisco, CA: HarperCollins Publishers Inc.

Chopra, D. (1993). *Ageless Body, Timeless Mind.* New York, NY. Harmony Books.

Csikszentmihalyi, M. (1997). *Finding Flow.* New York, NY: Basic Books.

Dennison, P. E., & Dennison, G. E. (1994). *Brain Gym: Teacher's Edition Revised.* Ventura, CA: Edu-Kinesthetics, Inc.

Faculty of the New City School (1994). *Celebrating Multiple Intelligences.* St. Louis, MO: The New City School, Inc.

Feldenkrais, M. (1972). *Awareness Through Movement.* New York, NY: Harper and Row Publishers.

Feldenkrais, M. (1979). *Body and Mature Behavior.* New York, NY: International Universities Press, Inc.

Feldenkrais, M. (1981). *The Elusive Obvious.* Cupertino, CA: Meta Publications.

Fisher, J. (1979). *Johnson and Johnson From Baby to Toddler.* New York, NY: Berkley Publishing Group.

Gardner, H. (1999) *Intelligence Reframed.* New York NY: Basic Books.

Goddard, S. (2002). Reflexes, Learning and Behavior: A Window into the Child's Mind. Eugene, OR: Fern

REFERENCES

Ridge Press.

Goldstein, B. (2010). *Sensation and Perception 8th Edition,* Belmont, CA: Wadsworth, Cengage Learning.

Goleman, D. (2006) *Emotional Intelligence,* New York, NY: Bantam Books.

Gustafson, D. (1980). *Physics: Health and the Human Body*. Belmont, CA: Wadsworth Publishing Company.

Guyton, A. (1974). *Function of the Human Body.* Philadelphia, PA: W. B. Saunders Company.

Hannaford, C. (2002). A*wakening the Child's Heart*. Captain Cook, HI: Jamilla Nur Publishing.

Hannaford, C. (2005). *Smart Moves 2nd Edition*. Salt Lake City, UT: Great River Books.

Houston, J. (1982). *The Possible Human*. Los Angeles, CA: J.P. Tarcher. Inc.

Jensen, E. (1998). *Teaching with the Brain in Mind*. Alexandria, VA: Association for Supervision and Curriculum Development.

Keleman, S. (1985). *Emotional Anatomy.* Berkeley, CA: Center Press.

Kephart, N.C. (1968). *Steps to Achievement for the Slow Learner.* Columbus, OH: Charles E. Merrill Publishing Company

Kondrot, E. C. (2000). *Healing the Eyes*. Carson City, NV: Nutritional Research Press.

Lavatelli, C. (1973). *Piaget's Theory Applied to an Early Childhood Curriculum*. Cambridge, MA: Center for Media Development, Inc. Book.

Levine, M. (2002). *A Mind at the Time*. New York, NY: Simon & Schuster Paperbacks.

Madigan, J. (2004). *Thinking on Your Feet*. Murphy, TX: Action Based Learning.

Medina, J. (2008). *Brain Rules.* Seattle, WA: Pear Press.

Neufeld, G., Maté, G. (2006). *Hold On to Your Kids*. New York, NY: Ballantine Books.

New City School. Inc. (1997). *Multiple Intelligences: Teaching for Success.* New York, NY: New York City School. Inc.

Pert, C. (1997). *Molecules of Emotion*. New York, NY: Scribner.

Pukui, Mary Kawena, Samuel H. Elbert (1986), *Hawaiian Dictionary*. Honolulu, HI: University of Hawaii Press.

Quackenbush, T. R. (1999). *Relearning to See: Improve Your Eyesight – Naturally!* Berkeley, CA: North Atlantic Books.

Randolph, S. and Heiniger, M. (1994). *Kids Learn from the Inside Out.* Boise, ID: Legendary Publishing Company.

Ratey, J. (2002). *A User's Guide to the Brain.* New York, NY: Pantheon Books.

Ratey. J (2008). *Spark, the Revolutionary New Science of Exercise and the Brain.* New York, NY: Little, Brown and Company.

Robinson, K. (2001). *Out of Our Minds: Learning To Be Creative.* Chichester, West Sussex, UK: Capstone Publishing Limited.

Rosenblum, Lawrence D. (2010), *See What I'm Saying.* New York, NY: W.W. Norton & Company, Inc.

Sherrington, Charles S. (1906). *The Integrative Action of the Nervous System.* New Haven, CT: Yale University Press.

Shenkin, D., Schachter, M. and Hutton, R. (1987). *Food, Mind and Mood.* New York, NY: Warner Book, Inc.

Stassen Berger, K. (2003). *The Developing Person.* New York, NY: Worth Publishers.

Stokes, B. (2002). *Amazing Babies, Essential Movement for Your Baby in the First Year.* Toronto, ON: Move Alive Media Inc.

Taylor, J. (2006). *My Stroke of Insight.* New York, NY; Penguin Group.

Thelen, E. and Smith, L (1996). *A Dynamic Systems Approach to the Development of Cognition and Action.* London, UK: The MIT Press.

ARTICLES AND WEBSITES

Barnes et al. (2003), Napoli et al. (2005), Schonert-Reichi and Miller (2005). Cited in "Infographic: Meditation Schools Across America." *Edutopia.* Retrieved July 2012, from http://www.edutopia.org/stw-student-stress meditation-schools-infographic

Centers For Disease Control (2007, September 8). "Teen Suicide Rate: Highest Increase in 15 Years." *Science Daily.* Retrieved August 6, 2012, from *http://www.sciencedaily.com/releases/2007/09/070907221530.htm*

Epstein, M., Atkins, M., Cullinan, R., Kutash, K., and Weaver, R. (2008). *Reducing Behavior Problems in the Elementary School Classroom: A Practice Guide.* National Center for Education Evaluations and Regional Assistance in conjunction with The Institute of Educational Sciences and The U.S. Department of Education. Retrieved August 2012, from *http://ies.ed.gov/ncee/wwc/publications/practiceguides*

Maté, G. (2010). "When the Body Says No: Understanding the Stress-Disease Connection." *Democracy*

Now. Retrieved February 15, 2010, from *http://www.democracynow.org/2010/2/15/dr_gabor_mat_when_ the body*

Moreno C., Laje G., Blanco C., Jiang H., Schmidt A.B., Olfson M. (2007). "National Trends in the Outpatient Diagnosis and Treatment of Bipolar Disorder in Youth." *Archives of General Psychiatry*, Vol 64, No. 9.

Nardo & Reynolds (2002). As cited in Peck, H. L., Kehle, T. J., Bray, M. A., & Theodore, L. A. (2005) "Yoga as an Intervention for Children With Attention Problems." *School Psychology Review*, V. 34, No. 3, pp. 415-424. Retrieved November 2006, from *http://www.yogaed.com/pdfs/yo_intervention_child_atten.pdf*

Ruth, P. W., Pert, C. (n.d.). "The Mind-Body Connection in Learning." *Trans4mind*. Retrieved Feb 21 2006, from *http://www.trans4mind.com/counterpoint/index-health-fitness/weiss.shtml*

Rosenberg, Marshall (2012)."What is NVC?" *The Center for Non-Violent Communication*. Retrieved July 2012, from *http://www.cnvc.org/about/what-is-nvc.html*

Smetacek, V., Mechsner, F. (Published online 3 November 2004). "Concept of Making Sense." *Nature* 2004 432:21.

Wallis, C., & Steptoe, S. (December 2006). "How to Bring Our Schools Out of the 20th Century." *Time Magazine*. Retrieved December 2006 from *http://www.time.com/time/magazine/article/0,9171,1568480,00. html*

INDEX

WELLNESS THROUGH MOVEMENT®

For General Support

Log on to www.WellnessThroughMovement.com to get on the mailing list for online notices about workshops, conference calls, and seminars.

For Unique Needs and Complex Conditions

PART II YOUNG AT HEART P.E. For the Heart, Body, and Mind: This in-depth series of twenty neuromuscular reeducation movement games is based on the *Feldenkrais Method®*, developmental movements, and the National Physical Education Standards for elementary grades. The program uses alignment, attitude, and quality of movement to expand perception. Games also target the physical and emotional challenges that narrow attention or fuel problem behaviors. *Young At Heart P.E.* organizes the stimulus of motor patterns that contribute to self-perception.

For Academic Support

PART III MOVEMENT FOR THE LEARNER In-Classroom Curriculum: This series of fifty-two in-classroom sensory-movement lessons is designed to enhance brain functioning and improve performance in language arts and mathematics. More important, the lessons aid in developing social skills, attention skills, and higher order skills. These lessons are designed to also increase physical comfort for people while seated at a desk or when they are required to have long attention spans. *Movement for the Learner In-Classroom Curriculum* integrates the studies of the *Feldenkrais Method®*, cognitive development theories, and stages of sensory-motor development.

65050532R00060

Made in the USA
Lexington, KY
29 June 2017